DATE DUE			
JAN 15 '66			
MAR 1 2 '66			
MAR 2 4 03 LIBRARY			
FEB 19 2001			
GAYLORD			PRINTED IN U.S.A.

THE SEVENTEENTH-CENTURY SHERIFF

The University of North Carolina Press
Chapel Hill, N. C.

The Baker and Taylor Co.
New York

Oxford University Press
London

Maruzen-Kabushiki-Kaisha
Tokyo

THE SEVENTEENTH-CENTURY SHERIFF

A COMPARATIVE STUDY OF THE SHERIFF
IN ENGLAND AND THE CHESAPEAKE COLONIES
1607-1689

CYRUS HARRELD KARRAKER, Ph.D.
Associate Professor of History, Birmingham-Southern College

CHAPEL HILL

THE UNIVERSITY OF NORTH CAROLINA PRESS

1930

COPYRIGHT, 1930, BY
THE UNIVERSITY OF NORTH CAROLINA PRESS

PRINTED IN THE UNITED STATES OF AMERICA BY
THE SEEMAN PRESS, DURHAM, NORTH CAROLINA

TO

MY FATHER AND MOTHER

PREFACE

It is generally accepted that the American Colonies of the seventeenth century derived their local political institutions from England and that such divergencies as arose were due mainly to environment. But how much of English institutional life was borrowed, and how much was found unadapted to the environment? Colonial local government was unquestionably of English origin, but the extent to which the administrative and judicial systems of England were consciously copied in the colonies, the nature of the divergencies that arose, the reasons for these divergencies, their breadth and ultimate importance constitute a field of research that has not yet been carefully worked.

Without a discussion of background the existing studies of local government in the colonies are incomplete. Many questions arise that are left unanswered. For example, though the descriptions of the colonial county court are detailed, one still feels impelled to seek its origin. The colonial county court resembled the English court of quarter-sessions, but how closely? To mention only one other of the numerous questions that arise: how nearly did the election system in Maryland correspond to that of England, from which it originated? Had pioneer conditions wrought important changes? We find little specific information in secondary works regarding the nature and extent of our institutional heritage from England and the manner of its reshaping by environment, though continuity and development stand out significantly in every volume of the orders of the county courts of Virginia and Maryland. It seems as difficult to interpret properly colonial local government with a perspective almost purely colonial as to understand Anglo-Norman local government apart from its Anglo-Saxon origins.

A study of the sheriff in England, Virginia, and Maryland involves a broader field of local government than that office itself, for the sheriff functioned in close contact with the governmental machinery of the county, the hundred, and the parish. For greater fullness and clarity of treatment, therefore, general descriptions of local institutions are given wherever appropriate. But a minute investigation of the courts, the assizes, and the quarter-sessions in England, or the county court, the general and the provincial courts in the colonies, and the offices of justice of the peace, coroner, county clerk, and other officials, seemed unnecessary and was not attempted.

The unpublished materials dealing with the English phase of the subject are abundant and are scattered widely throughout England. They are to be found in the national archives, in the records of the various counties, and in many private collections of documents. Only a small part of these unprinted sources of information have been indicated in the guides and bibliographies dealing with the subject. The discovery of manuscripts of value for this study, consequently, had to be largely a matter of chance.

The study of the colonial sheriff, on the other hand, involved different problems of research. They were not principally those of discovery and selection, as in the case of the English records, but of drawing all the information possible out of the scant lot of source materials that have been preserved. The orders and proceedings of the council in executive session, of the general, provincial, and county courts, together with the acts of the Assembly, comprise nearly all the printed and manuscript materials available. The volumes of records of the council, yet unprinted, are to be found in the state archives at Richmond and Annapolis; those of the county court, in the Virginia state archives and in the offices of the county or circuit clerks in more than a dozen county seats of Virginia and Maryland. Comparatively few court order books of the seventeenth century exist, and these were written by the clerks with such exceeding brevity as to draw heavily on the imagination of the student. Yet from the records of the courts and the council, together with the statutes, nearly all our information must come. The equally brief English court records and legal treatises are clarified and supplemented by autobiographies, letters, and journals, which furnish intimate revelations of the public life of the sheriff and his associates in office; but these, unfortunately, do not exist for the colonies. The colonial source materials, consequently, had to be drained dry; even so, there are gaps in the study that seem impossible to fill. Among the problems yet unsolved are the casual revenues in the colonies and their nature and importance as compared with other royal and proprietary revenues.

This study has been divided into three parts. Part I describes the office of sheriff in England; Part II, his position in Virginia and Maryland; Part III consists of documents, many previously unprinted, selected to illustrate the points of similarity and divergence discussed in the text and, to a certain degree, the workings of local government.

The present study was made possible through the assistance of my instructors in the University of Pennsylvania and of librarians and archivists in this country and in England. I am under the greatest obligation to Professor Edward P. Cheyney, of the University of Pennsylvania, who encouraged me to undertake this rather unusual study and who gave generously of both his time and his high scholarship to the search for materials and the reading of the manuscript. I wish also to express to Professor Herman V. Ames and Professor St. George L. Sioussat of the University of Pennsylvania my appreciation of their assistance in reading the manuscript. I owe much to Dr. H. R. McIlwaine, Virginia State Librarian, and to Mr. Morgan P. Robinson, State Archivist, for their untiring efforts and invaluable aid in the discovery and proper interpretation of council and court records. The officials of the Library of Congress and of the state historical societies were in like manner unfailingly helpful.

On the other side of the water, access was readily gained to archives, national and local, and to private repositories of documents. The custodian or owner in each case seemed anxious to be of the utmost possible service. While lack of space forbids mention of my obligations to each, I welcome the opportunity of acknowledging my debt to the officials of the Public Record Office, the British Museum, the Chetham Library in Manchester, and to Lord Kenyon, Vice-Chancellor of the University of Wales, who so generously permitted the examination of his most interesting and valuable collection of documents, for their close coöperation in this adventure.

CYRUS H. KARRAKER

Birmingham-Southern College
Birmingham, Alabama.

CONTENTS

PART I
THE SHERIFF IN ENGLAND

	PAGE
PREFACE	vii

I. QUALIFICATIONS AND APPOINTMENT... 3
Property Qualifications—Residence in the County—Loyalty—Other Restrictions—Method of Appointment—Petitions for Relief—Seeking Appointment—Admission to Office—The Sheriff's Officials: Spoils of Office—The Under-Sheriff.

II. COURT SERVICE 14
The Oath of Office—Two Types of Duties—Organization of Quarter-Sessions and Assizes—Impanelling Juries—Chief Executive Official—Quasi-Judicial Activity—Police Power—Military Duties—Social Distinction—Entertaining at the Assizes—Administrative Work of the Assizes—Selection of a Chaplain.

III. AS A CHANNEL OF GOVERNMENTAL COMMUNICATION 29
Publication of Proclamations—Election Responsibilities—Election Worries—As General Intermediary—As Temporary Treasurer.

IV. THE SHERIFF'S COUNTY COURT.......... 37
Importance of the County Court—The Middleton Case—Court Membership and Procedure—*Bigland* vs. *Langdale*—The Sheriff as Chairman and Executive—Jurisdiction of the County Court—Defects of the County Court.

V. FINANCIAL DUTIES 53
Collector of Prerogative Revenues—King Versus Parliament—Benevolences—Forced Loans and Compositions for Knighthood—Collection of Ship-Money—General Deductions.

PART II
THE SHERIFF IN THE CHESAPEAKE COLONIES

VI. QUALIFICATIONS AND APPOINTMENT... 63
Early Conditions in Virginia—Provost-Marshal, Forerunner of the Sheriff—Duties of the Provost-Marshal—Early Provost-Marshals and Sheriffs—Property Qualifications — Other Restrictions — Method of Appointment—Admission to Office—Irregularities and Grievances—The Under-Sheriff—Other Officials—Maryland a Proprietary Province—The Office of Commander—Formation of Counties—The Hundred as a Governmental Unit—County Government in Maryland—The Sheriff in Maryland—The Case of Edward Sweatman—Appointment and Induction—Leadership of the Sheriff in Maryland.

VII. COURT SERVICE 93
The Oath of Office—Organization of Courts—Impanelling of Juries—Chief Executive Official—As Administrative Official—Court Duties in Maryland—Dignity of Court Officials—Comparison with England—Reasons for Legal and Institutional Divergencies—Court Procedure Modeled After England—Advantages of Freer Environment.

VIII. AS A CHANNEL OF GOVERNMENTAL COMMUNICATION 114
Publication of Proclamations—Election Responsibilities—Governmental Communication in Maryland—Significance of the Hundred—Comparison with England.

IX. FINANCIAL DUTIES 130
Collector of Poll Taxes—Method of Taxation—Collector's Fees—Collector of King's Revenues—Deodands—Tax Collector in Maryland—Proprietary Revenues—The Sheriff's Accounting—Comparison with England.

X. CONSERVATOR OF THE PEACE: CONCLUSION 147
Police Powers—Enforcing Political Conformity—Enforcing Religious Conformity—General Summary

—Divergencies from England—Lack of Judicial Functions—Election Divergencies—Colonial County More Independent—Sheriff More Independent—Sheriff More Democratic: More Important—The Sheriff as an Institution.

PART III
ILLUSTRATIVE DOCUMENTS

ILLUSTRATIVE DOCUMENTS 163
1. The Patent of the Sheriff's Office, England—2. Patent of Office, Virginia, 1684—3. The Sheriff's Patent of Assistance, England—4. Oath of Office Taken by Sheriff William Ffarington, England, 1636—5. The Sheriff's Oath of Office, Virginia, 1641—6. The Sheriff's Oath of Office, Maryland, 1642—7. Jailer's Bond to Sheriff, England, 1636—8. Writ of Election, England, 1603—9. Writ of Election, Maryland, 1670—10. The Sheriff to Collect Salary of Parochial Burgess, Virginia—11. The Sheriff to Supervise Election of the Vestry, Virginia—12. Warrant for Summoning the Posse Comitatus, England, 1643—13. Warrant from the Justices of the Peace to the Sheriff to Summon the Sessions, England, 1624—14. Commission of the Peace, England—15. Commission of the Peace, Maryland, 1681—16. Description of a Procession to the Assizes, England—17. The Sheriff's Writ of Discharge, England—18. Rotation of Office, Virginia, 1668-69—19. Military Command Given to the Sheriff, Maryland, 1648—20. The Coroner to Summon the Sheriff, Maryland, 1684—21. The Sheriff's Warrant to Take the List of Tithables, Maryland, 1666—22. A Typical Writ with the Sheriff's Return—23. The Sheriff and Coroners to Recover the Crown's Casual Revenues, Virginia, 1700—24. Deodand—25. Commission of the Commander, Virginia, 1626—26. Oath of the County Clerk, Virginia, 1673-74—27. Oath of the Constable, Virginia, 1640-45.

BIBLIOGRAPHY 198

INDEX 215

PART I
THE SHERIFF IN ENGLAND

Chapter I
QUALIFICATIONS AND APPOINTMENT
Property Qualifications

A LONG LIST of statutes, dating from the reign of Edward II, confined the office of sheriff to those having sufficient property to answer the King.[1] These statutes were intended to secure the responsibility of the sheriff, but other financial requirements of the office—the heavy expenses entailed at his entry into office, in entertaining the judges and country gentry at the assizes, and in the process of accounting into the Exchequer—likewise necessitated the sheriff's being a member of the wealthier class in the county. It was from this class, the country gentry, which filled the more important county offices except that of lord-lieutenant and elected to Parliament out of their number the "knights of the shire," that the sheriffs were almost always chosen. Dalton informs us on the title-page of the standard work on the sheriff in the seventeenth century that his book is written "for the better encouragement of the Gentrie upon whom the burthen of the Office lyeth."[2] A member of this class is appointed justice of the peace of the county; later, its sheriff; and, after serving his year, is often found back again on the county bench while another of the justices has taken his place as sheriff. The list of justices of the peace for the

---

[1] 9 Ed. II; 2 Ed. III, c. 4; 4 Ed. III, c. 9; 5 Ed. III, c. 4; 14 Car. II, c. 21.
[2] Michael Dalton, *Officium Vicecomitum, or the Office and Authorities of Sheriffs.*

county of Somerset from 1660 to 1685, compared with a list of its sheriffs, shows that the two offices in that county were filled by practically the same persons, and these were all members of the country gentry.[3] Among distinguished Englishmen of the seventeenth century who served the two offices successively were the father of John Evelyn, who at the time of his shrievalty was worth £4,000 a year, and Anthony Ashley Cooper.[4]

Residence in the County

An important restriction on the choice of sheriff, but more of a restriction on his personal activities, was that of residence in his county. By the statute of 4 Henry IV, c. 5, the sheriff was to be sworn in his oath of office to dwell in his county "excepte ye be otherwise licensed by the king." That this requirement was a considerable vexation to practically all holding the office is evident from the many petitions to the King that sprinkle the records (or, during the Interregnum, to Parliament), for permission to leave the county. Certain sheriffs wished to be absent for a time on business trips to London and elsewhere; others, throughout the term of office, because their homes were in other counties. One petitioner stated that he had been sheriff of Leicester for the year ending at Michaelmas and, being appointed

[3] *Quarter Sessions Records for The County of Somerset*, IV, viii-xxi; Public Record Office, *Lists and Indexes*, No. IX—a check-list of the sheriffs of England and Wales to 1831. (Hereafter referred to as *Lists and Indexes*, No. IX.)

[4] John Evelyn, *Diary*, 1639; W. D. Christie, *A Life of Anthony Ashley Cooper, First Earl of Shaftesbury, Diary*, 1646, 1647.

QUALIFICATIONS AND APPOINTMENT 5

sheriff of Stafford for the ensuing year, prayed license to reside in Leicester.[5] A person might be appointed for any county in which he had a sufficient estate,[6] but he was not forced by the appointment to move his home to that county for the year. The practice on such occasions was for the appointee to secure permission to live in his home county and, this being received, to discharge the duties of his office in the county to which he was appointed mainly through his under-sheriff. The following illustration seems typical: when Sir William Selby, the younger, appointed sheriff of Northumberland for 1604, requested leave from the King to reside with his family in Kent, James wrote to his chancellor, Lord Ellesmere, ordering him not to compel Selby to stay all the time in Northumberland to execute his office but to allow him to execute it there partly by himself and partly by his deputies.[7] Probably the best known instance of the strict application of the residence requirement occurred in 1625, when Charles I rid himself of seven of the leaders of the opposition in Parliament by appointing them sheriffs. Sir Edward Coke and Sir Thomas Wentworth were two of the number thus disabled, the former becoming "the ruler" of Buckinghamshire and the latter "the great Officer of Yorkshire."[8]

[5] *Calendar of State Papers, Domestic, 1629-31*, p. 463.
[6] *Ibid., 1676-77*, p. 412.
[7] *The Egerton Papers*, pp. 389-90; see also *Journals of the House of Commons*, IV, 425.
[8] *Calendar of State Papers, Domestic, 1625-26*, p. 132; C. W. Johnson, *The Life of Sir Edward Coke*, II, 169; *The Earl of Strafforde's Letters and Dispatches*, I, 29.

Loyalty

During the civil wars Parliament took special pains to appoint those loyal to it.[9] It was for this reason that Humphrey Chetham, a prominent merchant and landowner of Manchester, was appointed sheriff of Lancashire for the year 1649, though incapacitated by old age and sickness and yet, unluckily for him, considered by Parliament its only supporter in the county qualified to discharge the duties of the office.[10]

Other Restrictions

Another restriction on the office prohibited the sheriff from serving at the same time as justice of the peace, because he would then be executing his own orders.[11] He likewise was forbidden to act as an attorney in the courts he served.[12] Nor could the sheriff or under-sheriff serve again in such capacity until after the lapse of three years, unless there were no other in the county of sufficient property,[13] although, as noticed above, he might be appointed to the shrievalty in another county the following year if possessed of a sufficient freehold there.

Method of Appointment

With the exception of the County Palatine of Durham, where the sheriff was appointed by the

[9] *Acts and Ordinances of the Interregnum, 1642-1660,* I, 373 (Jan., 1643-44); *ibid.,* p. 1009 (Sept., 1647); *Journals of the House of Commons,* III, 712; *Gloucestershire Notes and Queries,* V, 36.
[10] *Life of Humphrey Chetham,* pp. 175-76.
[11] P. and M., St. 2, C. 8. (*Statutes of the Realm.*)
[12] Henry V, c. 4.
[13] Richard II, c. 11; 23 Henry VI, c. 7.

QUALIFICATIONS AND APPOINTMENT 7

Bishop, and of Westmoreland, where his appointment was a hereditary right of the Cliffords,[14] the sheriffs of all the English counties were appointed in the following manner: every year on the first of November certain of the higher government officials met in special session with the Council in the Exchequer and there chose lists of three persons for each county who seemed best qualified for the office; these lists were then submitted to the King who "pricked" one out of each, who thereupon secured their letters patent and took their oaths as sheriffs.[15]

During the Interregnum important changes were made in the process of presenting and appointing: the names of those qualified in each county were presented by the county members, and appointment was made by ordinance of Parliament.[16] During this period the Bishop of Durham lost his right of appointment, but the hereditary right in Westmoreland was left unmolested.

Each county after 1575 had its own sheriff with the exception of Surrey and Sussex, which were joined under one sheriff until 1636, and Cambridge and Huntingdon, which were combined throughout

[14] *Lists and Indexes,* No. IX; *Virginia Magazine of History and Biography,* I, 275.

[15] Fortescue, *De Laudibus Legum Angliae,* chap. XXIV. But who gave the names to the Council? In 1636 the Council, in letters to the Chancellor of the Duchy of Lancaster and to the judges of assize, requested lists of four or more of the ablest persons in their counties fit to be high sheriffs.—*Calendar of State Papers, Domestic, 1636-37,* p. 123. This seems to have been the customary method for many years afterward.

[16] *Journals of the House of Commons,* III, 688, 711, 712; IV, 425; VII, 193, etc.

the period except for the short interval between 1636 in 1643, when a sheriff was appointed annually for each.[17]

PETITIONS FOR RELIEF

The method of appointment, though arbitrary, did not preclude the high government officials and the King or Parliament from hearing petitions from those anxious to be spared or relieved of the heavy responsibilities and exhausting expenses of the office. Humphrey Chetham, hearing in 1634 that he was to be appointed, wrote to a friend pleading with him "if anie putt me forward" to "stand in the waie and suffer mee not to come in the ranke of those that shall be presented to the King's view."[18] After the lists were made up other requests came to the King or to Parliament for sparing certain nominees;[19] and finally, after choice had been made, came affidavits of incapacity, accompanied by lists of persons better qualified, from the petitioners in support of their prayers for release from the burdensome office.[20] Humphrey Chetham, who, as we have noticed, was pressed into his country's service again in 1649 as sheriff of Lancashire, went to even greater trouble than in 1634 to save himself, and, as it turned out, with better success. He assured the speaker of the House that upon hearing of his appointment he had written to the members from Lancashire then in London, and his friends had written to the speaker

[17] *Lists and Indexes*, No. IX.
[18] *Life of Humphrey Chetham*, p. 74.
[19] John Evelyn, *Diary*, Nov. 6, 1663.
[20] *Calendar of State Papers, Domestic, 1625-26*, p. 156.

QUALIFICATIONS AND APPOINTMENT 9

affirming his inability to serve because of old age and infirmity; also that the truth had been made known by letters and certificates from the gentlemen of the county and by his physician. He prayed that the House be acquainted with these facts that they might appoint some other better qualified.[21] Chetham was relieved of his burden, but when his successor, a certain Hartley, also tried to escape by pleading poverty and, that excuse failing, even planned to submit to a fine and imprisonment rather than serve as sheriff, he was persuaded from his course by a warning to desist or else the House would punish him severely by way of example to others.[22]

Some of the petitions of this character were granted, though probably not many, success or failure depending largely on the degree of influence exercised by the petitioner's friends at court,[23] or in Parliament as in the case of Chetham.

Seeking Appointment

On the other hand, there were those, though much less frequently mentioned, who sought appointment. There was Sir John Reresby, the famous traveler. We learn that Charles II had granted him the shrievalty as a compensation for losses sustained in his and his father's service, but unfortunately the county had been so impoverished by the many disturbances that the office had proved a loss to him instead of a profit. Reresby promised a large reward to a cer-

[21] *Life of Humphrey Chetham*, pp. 169-70.
[22] *Ibid.*, pp. 184-85.
[23] *Calendar of State Papers, Domestic, 1625-26*, p. 151.

tain Williamson should the latter succeed, through Lord Arlington, in persuading the King to continue him in office another year.[24]

Admission to Office

There seems to have been no general requirement that the sheriff go to Westminster for any part of the proceedings relating to his admission to office. The letters patent of his office, a commission giving him custody of the county and specifically requiring the accounting of the Crown revenues into the Exchequer, were, on one occasion, sent him by a messenger whose expenses the sheriff himself had to pay;[25] and, at another time, were given to him by four of the country gentry commissioned to administer his oath of office.[26] Bond to secure his financial responsibilities was taken by government officials who happened to be in the county at the time, or by some of the gentry,[27] of whom two or three also became his sureties.[28] His oath of office and the oaths of Supremacy and Allegiance were usually taken in the county before several justices of the peace by authority of a special commission from the Chancery.[29] The final step of admission to the duties of

[24] *Ibid.*, *1667*, p. 489.
[25] "Order of the Privy Council," *Calendar of State Papers, Domestic, 1637*, p. 448.
[26] *Exchequer—King's Remembrancer: List of Sheriffs' Accounts*, bundle 14/33.
[27] *Ibid.*, bundle 60/15.
[28] *The Earl of Strafforde's Letters and Dispatches*, I, 29.
[29] Dalton, *Officium Vicecomitum*, cap. 2. Of the five persons appointed to administer the oath of office to William Ffarington in 1635, two were to be of the quorum, and they were to make return of their proceedings to the Duchy Chamber at Westminster.—Raines MSS, XXIII, 73.

QUALIFICATIONS AND APPOINTMENT

the office was effected by issuance of the writ of discharge to the incumbent, which commanded him to transfer to the newly-appointed sheriff all the prisoners and writs, as well as all the official records in his keeping.[30] This transfer might be made formally before the freeholders assembled in the county court.

THE SHERIFF'S OFFICIALS: SPOILS OF OFFICE

At the first county court, after the giving over of the writ of discharge, the sheriff read his patent of office and his writ of assistance, which together conferred unlimited authority in the county, and appointed his officials: the under-sheriff, the county clerk, and four or more bailiffs.[31] The sheriff was subjected to much advice and importunity in filling these positions and others, the offices in the sheriff's gift being in far greater demand than the shrievalty itself. To Sir Thomas Wentworth, one of the group excluded from Parliament in 1625, a friend recommended a kinsman as well qualified by experience for the office of under-sheriff, and another suggested a Mr. Blanch as a wise choice for his jailer at York Castle.[32] Early in December, 1648,[33] when it seemed that Humphrey Chetham could not possibly escape the office, Ralph Assheton recommended to him a good man for his under-sheriff, another for

[30] J. Wilkinson, *Treatise . . . concerning the Office and Authoritie of Coroners and Sherifes*, p. 5.
[31] *Loc. cit.*
[32] *The Earl of Strafforde's Letters and Dispatches*, I, 30-31.
[33] The dates given in the text and footnotes are Old Style.

his clerk, and another for "ye exigenturs place."[34] A friend wrote to him at the request of one who wanted to be his bailiff, and still another was put forward as a candidate for the clerkship.[35]

THE UNDER-SHERIFF

Among all the sheriff's officials, including the keeper of the sheriff's seal, the most important and most useful was the under-sheriff or deputy sheriff. The under-sheriff was expected to know some law, "especially if the sheriff be not learned himselfe."[36] Ellesmere, in November, 1606, recommended to the sheriff of the county of Southampton the bearer, "one Brian Chamberlayne, a man of good yeeres, judgment and discretion, and that hath spent him time in the studye of the lawe."[37] Humphrey Chetham must have been badly informed as to the qualifications of his appointee, for the bad legal advice of this person caused him considerable trouble with the Crown.[38] Sir Thomas Wentworth, on the other hand, perhaps not needing to be so dependent on another for knowledge of the law, declared to a friend that in order to cut expenses he would execute the under-sheriffwick by his own servants.[39]

The under-sheriff was a sworn official and under

[34] It was the duty of the "exigentur" to demand by proclamation in the sheriff's county court the appearance of one who failed to appear, on pain of outlawry.
[35] *Life of Humphrey Chetham*, pp. 161-63.
[36] Sir Thomas Smith, *De Republica Anglorum*, bk. II, chap. 17.
[37] Historical Manuscripts Commission, *Report VII*, Appendix, p. 668.
[38] *Life of Humphrey Chetham*, pp. 86-88.
[39] *The Earl of Strafforde's Letters and Dispatches*, I, 32.

QUALIFICATIONS AND APPOINTMENT 13

bond like the bailiffs and jailer to perform the duties of his office, for which he was to receive certain fees. While several statutes prohibited the under-sheriff's being reappointed the three years following, in an effort to diminish his opportunities for extortion, these laws seem to have been poorly enforced, some under-sheriffs serving for three or more successive years.[40] The under-sheriff is rarely to be found filling the office of justice of the peace or that of sheriff.

Inasmuch as the county clerk and the bailiffs will be discussed in succeeding chapters, nothing need be said about their duties at this time. As for the jailer, the sheriff had the keeping of the county jail and its prisoners and was answerable for the keepers he put in its charge.[41]

[40] See the names of the under-sheriffs in the *North Riding of the County of York Quarter-Sessions Records,* vols. IV and V.

[41] 14 Ed. III, c. 10; 19 Henry VIII, c. 10. The jailer of William Ffarington gave him bond for £1,000 (see *infra,* Illustrative Documents, No. 7).

Chapter II
COURT SERVICE
The Oath of Office

MANY OF the duties of the sheriff are enumerated in his oath of office. William Ffarington, sheriff of Lancashire in 1636, was sworn to perform the following services: to protect the King's rights and account for the King's debts; to serve and return the King's writ "as far forth as itt shalbee in yor cunninge"; to do all in his power to destroy heresies within his bailiwick, and to assist the commissaries and ordinaries in church matters; to execute the statutes against felonies; to make his panels himself; to do right to poor as well as rich; not to let his sheriffwick or bailiwick to farm to any man; to choose his bailiffs of true and sufficient men for whom he was to be responsible, and not to choose his under-sheriff or sheriff's clerk of the preceding year; to be resident within his county during his term of office;[1] and finally, to make a true account of all the profits and casualties of the office during his term.[2]

Except for a few slight changes this was the oath taken by the sheriffs throughout the period. In 1625, Sir Edward Coke, struggling against his removal by Charles I from the House of Commons to the shrievalty, protested the part of the oath that required him to destroy heresies, called "Lollories,"

[1] Most of the oaths of office add, "unless ye be otherwise licensed by the King."
[2] *The Shrievalty of William Ffarington,* pp. 1-3.

on the ground that he would thereby be compelled to suppress the established religion since "Lollard" was but another name for "Protestant." His objection was sustained by the judges and this requirement thereafter omitted from the oath.[3] Another change, though lasting no longer than the Interregnum, was effected by an ordinance of 1643/44, which substituted "Lords and Commons" for "the King" in the licensing part of the residence clause.[4]

Two Types of Duties

The duties of the office of sheriff may, for the sake of convenience of study, be grouped into two large classes: one consisting of those functions which had continued useful during the centuries of the development of county government, and which were being added to in this period by parliamentary enactments and by a series of orders from the Privy Council; and the other, of those remaining as little more than vestiges of the once important administrative and judicial functions of the mediaeval shrievalty. In the first class may be included the duties of the sheriff as the executive official of the courts, as a principal medium of communication between the central government and the county, and as a conservator of the peace; in the second, his work as the King's bailiff in enforcing the King's rights, collecting and accounting for his personal revenues, and keeping the county court. Before describing the duties of the

[3] C. W. Johnson, *The Life of Sir Edward Coke*, II, 170-71.
[4] *Acts and Ordinances of the Interregnum, 1642-1660*, I, 373-74.

sheriff a distinction should be made between the duties of the office as a whole and the personal activities of the sheriff. In general, either the high sheriff or his under-sheriff might supervise or in person perform the ministerial or routine work of the office; but there were certain other kinds of duties requiring the exercise of some judgment or the display of the greatness of the office, which belonged fundamentally to the high sheriff in person.

ORGANIZATION OF QUARTER-SESSIONS AND ASSIZES

On command of two or more justices of the peace, one being of the quorum, the sheriff notified the county of the place and date of the next quarter-sessions. By his own warrant he ordered his bailiff in each hundred to summon twenty-four men from that hundred to serve as jurors, and to notify all justices of the peace, coroners, stewards, constables, and bailiffs to be present with the records of their offices.[5] The sheriff himself only infrequently attended the sessions.[6] Presided over, as it was, by his quite familiar associates in public as in private life, the justices of the peace, the court did not inspire the

[5] *Worcestershire County Records, Calendar of the Quarter-Sessions Papers,* I, xci. Most writs specifically required the constables and others to hand in to the justices lists of artificers, laborers, and servants who had taken excessive wages contrary to law.—*Quarter-Sessions Records of the County of Northampton,* I, 4-5; Lancashire Indictments, Quarter-Sessions, Oct., 1657. At Epiphany, 1642-3, the sheriff of Devonshire was fined £100 for neglect of duty in not arranging for the sessions.—A. H. A. Hamilton, *Quarter-Sessions from Queen Elizabeth to Queen Anne,* p. 128.

[6] See *West Riding Sessions Records* and *North Riding of the County of York Quarter-Sessions Records* for the period.

sheriff with awe. Before the judges from Westminster holding the assizes he felt some constraint, but the court held by his neighbors he attended or neglected, apparently as he pleased. In addition, the court of quarter-sessions lacked those social and ceremonial functions that compelled the attendance of the sheriff on the more august assembly. In event of the absence of the high sheriff his under-sheriff impanelled the juries, produced the prisoners, and performed various other duties in his stead.

The organization of the assizes was accomplished in like manner by the sheriff's proclamation throughout his county that all officials and others with business at the court appear before the King's judges at a specified time and place.[7]

IMPANELLING JURIES

The sheriff impanelled all juries, and his frequent injudicious making of the panels—the giving of general summonses and the choosing of the unfit—was a cause for much criticism of the office during this period. In an effort to remedy these evils the Chancellor of the Duchy of Lancaster ordered the justices and sheriff of the county to make up freehold books containing the names of those in the county qualified to serve on juries. These lists were to guide the sheriff in making his panels; they were to be passed on to his successor and revised every so often.[8] Complaints were numerous, and else-

[7] *Acts and Ordinances of the Interregnum, 1642-1660*, I, 857; II, 518; Sheriff's Lists of Grand Juries, 1627-28; Assizes, 35/82, Order Book, 1640.

[8] Historical Manuscripts Commission, *Report XIV*, Appendix, pt. IV, p. 31.

where similar remedies were tried. At the Somerset assizes in March, 1637/8, the judges ordered the justices with others of the county to have the bailiffs of the hundreds hand in lists of the freeholders in every parish; from these the justices were to make up other lists of those fit to serve as jurors, and the sheriff was then to enter such lists in a freehold book from which thereafter he should make his panels. After their selection the jurors were to be notified by ticket from the bailiffs containing the names of the plaintiff and defendant or the cause for which they were summoned.[9]

CHIEF EXECUTIVE OFFICIAL

Besides organizing the King's courts in his county, the sheriff executed their orders, judgments, and sentences. He was their chief executive official. The execution and return of writs issuing from the local courts and from those at Westminster ordinarily comprised the bulk of the work of the office. Most of this routine work was, of necessity, given over by the sheriff to his officials, who were usually lowborn and so poorly paid in fees for their services as to be under constant temptation to plunder the people they visited. As expressed by the contemporary lawyer and writer, Dalton, "although the Sherife himselfe bee a man of especiall note and worth and his office of great authoritie and trust, yet wee see by dayly experience that all or most part of the Kings writs are served and executed by their undersherifes and Bailifes, which most commonly are per-

[9] Assizes 24/21, Order Book, 1641-52.

sons of small worth and account."[10] The statutes of Henry V, c. 4, and of 27 Elizabeth, c 12, had been passed to end the wholesale thievery of the sheriff's officials. Yet in addition to the above testimony we have from two other contemporary writers of legal textbooks, as well as from numerous complaints to the courts, the most vigorous condemnation of their rascality in deceiving the sheriff and robbing the people.[11] Here we find the chief defect in the sheriff's office—the performance of most of its duties by irresponsible under-officials. Indeed, the dishonesty and general unreliability of bailiffs, constables, and other small officials, and not of their superiors, the sheriff and justices of the peace, seems to have constituted the chief weakness in English local government during the Stuart period.

The sheriff executed a varied lot of orders from quarter-sessions and the assizes. In addition to the frequent orders to arrest, to imprison, to set at liberty, to produce in court or to take good security to appear at the next court, and to exact in his county court, are the following: to send wandering rogues into the next county; to send those convicted of petty larceny to the constables to be whipped; to hang those found guilty of felonies; and to burn in the market-place all relics of popery.[12] Other court duties

[10] Dalton, *Officium Vicecomitum,* cap. 94.
[11] Wilkinson, *Treatise ... concerning the Office and Authoritie of Coroners and Sherifes,* pp. 97, 107; William Greenwood, *A Practical Demonstration of County-Judicatures,* etc., pp. 11, 26. (Hereafter referred to as *County Court.*)
[12] July, 1656. *North Riding of the County of York Quarter-Sessions Records,* V, 220-21.

were civil in their nature: to put certain persons in possession of their lands; to attach for the security of a debt; to levy execution for the amount of a debt; to preside over appraisals and to return inventories of such; to collect the fines of quarter-sessions and from them to pay the justices their wages; and to pay each grand juror his expenses while attending court.[13] For the performance of court orders and other types of executive work the sheriff was paid the customary fees.

QUASI-JUDICIAL ACTIVITY

Not all the duties imposed on the sheriff by the courts were ministerial. There seems to have been much administrative or quasi-judicial work assigned to the sheriff either alone or associated with two or more justices of the peace or judges. For example, at the assizes held at Exeter in August, 1652, it was ordered, with the consent of the parties concerned, that all matters between them be referred "to the arbitrem^t of William Morrice Esq., sheriff of this County, who is desired to hear & determine the same."[14] At the Somerset assizes held in July, 1632, the high sheriff was appointed one of a committee of three to examine all those who had any grievances against a certain Lashbrooke and to certify the court at the next meeting "that an exemplary punishment may be inflicted upon him."[15] At the assizes for Somerset in August, 1629, two of

[13] *Ibid.*, p. 222.
[14] Assizes, 24/22, Order Book, 1652-76.
[15] Assizes, 24/20, Order Book, 1629-41.

the judges certified that they, with Sir John Stowell, sheriff of the county, had examined James Priest, committed for "speaking words concerning his Majesty's person."[16] The justices of the peace in session at Taunton in July, 1624, ordered John Stowell, one of their number, and Williams Francis, high sheriff, to call before them the inhabitants of two parishes and examine the "settling of John Trot";[17] and still more worthy of our attention is the command given to Sir John Hungerford, sheriff of Wiltshire, to join a number of the country gentry appointed at the summer assizes for Wiltshire to view the decay of Bradford's Bridge, to inquire what the repair of said bridge would amount to, what the town of Bradford could contribute, and to certify their findings at the next assizes.[18]

POLICE POWER

In still other matters of county administration the sheriff frequently acted as an associate of the justices of the peace. Though the justices were the chief administrators, the Privy Council usually addressed their letters regarding county administration to both justices and sheriff. The Council was equally dependent on the sheriff and the justices for the capture of criminals and for the suppression and investigation of disorders in various parts of the county. They were directed, from time to time, to coöperate

---

[16] *Calendar of State Papers, Domestic, 1629-31,* p. 39.
[17] *Quarter-Sessions Records for the County of Somerset,* I, 346.
[18] 1632. Assizes, 24/20, Order Book, 1629-41.

in breaking up meetings of Quakers, in searching recusants for weapons, and in quelling and seizing rioters and other disturbers of law and order.[19] The vast police powers of the sheriff were authorized by his commission and by his writ of assistance, the latter clothing him with power sufficient to call to the aid of himself and his deputies the *posse comitatus* consisting of all able-bodied men in the county.[20] In some emergencies, apparently without discrimination, the trained bands under the command of the deputy lieutenants were sent to his assistance.[21]

Military Duties

Though the military command in the counties during the Stuart period was exercised by the lord lieutenant and his deputies, some of the sheriff's activities were of a military character. In this regard, as in others, the division of duties between the higher county officials was never as clear-cut as statutes and legal textbooks indicate. The sheriff was often appointed one of the commissioners of musters,[22] and during the civil wars both King and Parliament

[19] *Journals of the House of Lords, 1660-66,* p. 154; *Acts of the Privy Council, 1613-14,* p. 556; *Calendar of State Papers, Domestic, 1658-59,* p. 363.

[20] *Quarter-Sessions Records for the County of Somerset,* III, 22; *Journals of the House of Commons,* II, 820; Hamilton, *Quarter-Sessions from Queen Elizabeth to Queen Anne,* p. 231. In emergencies the sheriff still summons the *posse* in the United States.

[21] *Calendar of State Papers, Domestic, 1627-28,* p. 292; *ibid., 1631-33,* p. 168; *Journals of the House of Commons,* II, 1000.

[22] *Acts of the Privy Council, 1601-4,* p. 505; *ibid., 1613-14,* pp. 119-20; Partington MSS, *Military Annals of Lancaster,* p. 64.

habitually commanded the sheriffs to rally the counties to their support as though military command were still theirs, *ex officio*.²³

Social Distinction

We have noticed that the central government depended on the close coöperation of the sheriff and justices of the peace for efficient county government. In social distinction the sheriff ranked above the justices of the peace. He was, even as late as the seventeenth century, still "the great man" of the county and as such on ceremonial occasions took precedence over other civil officials of the county. The high dignity of his office and the popular respect accorded him may be to some extent appreciated from glimpses of the sheriff on those gala days when the King's judges were in town. His brilliant regalia and lavish hospitality to the judges and country gentry at the assizes distinctly impressed all beholders. Sir Simonds D'Ewes relates that "on Tuesday, July the 6th, [1624], our High Sheriff going from Kediton to Bury St. Edmunds in the morning, I accompanied him thither, many other of the gentry of the shire meeting him on the way and attending him also. After we had dined with him, we likewise accompanied him in the afternoon, going out to meet the judges that were coming to keep the assizes at Bury."²⁴ William Ffarington when sheriff was

---

²³ Partington MSS, pp. 63, 64; *Tracts Relating to Military Proceedings in Lancashire During the Great Civil War*, pp. 7-8.

²⁴ *Autobiography and Correspondence of Sir Simonds D'Ewes,* I, 250.

even fined for not meeting the judges at a certain spot to escort them into the county town, although it is probable that they found this simply a convenient pretext for voicing displeasure with his economy in their entertainment. Humphrey Chetham, in 1635, was as conscientious in upholding the traditional ceremonies of his office, as he was in performing its duties. We are told that he and the judges rode on horseback, accompanied by the county magistrates, and in the procession were halberd-men and others amounting to nearly one hundred wearing the sheriff's livery, preceded by trumpeters "in Scarfs and Ribbons." In this formal procession they entered the county town and were there met by the mayor and aldermen. As Humphrey Chetham rode along he generously distributed doles to the bell-ringers at Garstang, to the poor at Preston, to the waits at Lancaster, and to the poor prisoners in the Castle.[25] Anthony Ashley Cooper informs us that at the spring assizes in 1647 he had sixty-six men in liveries;[26] and John Evelyn says that his father when sheriff had "116 servants in liverys, every one liveryed in greene sattin doublets; divers gentlemen and persons of quality waited on him in the same garb and habit, which at that time (when thirty or forty was the usual retinue of the High Sheriff) was esteem'd a great matter." Evelyn protests that his father outdid others in splendor not because of vanity, but because he could not refuse the civility of his friends

[25] Chetham MSS and Memoirs, pp. 44-45.
[26] W. D. Christie, *A Life of Anthony Ashley Cooper, First Earl of Shaftesbury*, pp. 82-83.

and relations who either came themselves or sent in their servants.[27]

Entertaining at the Assizes

The preparations for entertaining the judges and country gentry at the assizes were most elaborate. Humphrey Chetham wore rich gold lace, his best velvet suit, lace collar and shoe rosettes, along with "hat and feather."[28] Sir John Reresby, during the Lent assizes in 1667, "took a house" where he entertained "all comers" for ten days, his friends sending him between two and three hundred liveries. He kept two coaches, one for himself, the other for his under-sheriff, had his own violins there and "gave a ball and entertainment to all the ladies of the town" —the total cost amounting to over three hundred pounds. His expenses at the summer assizes were as great, and yet during his term he saved two hundred pounds.[29] Just how he managed so well is not stated. William Ffarington did his best to economize and yet felt constrained to employ a total of fifty-six helpers in his house during the summer assizes, comprising a steward, clerk of the kitchen, two yeomen of the plate cupboard, a yeoman of the wine cellar, two attendants in the sheriff's chamber, an usher of the hall, two chamberlains, four butchers and assistants, eight cooks, five scullions, a porter, caterer, slaughterman, poulterer, two watchmen for the horses, two to attend the docket door, and twenty

[27] Evelyn, *Diary*, 1634.
[28] Chetham MSS and Memoirs, p. 45.
[29] *Memoirs and Travels of Sir John Reresby, Bart.*, p. xvii.

to take turns at watching the prisoners.[30] An itemized expense account of a sheriff for one of the assizes in 1685 includes £ 38 for a new coach, £ 1 for "musick," £ 5 for a suit of clothes, £ 4 for preaching, over £ 6 in doles to the bell-ringers and poor, over £ 7 in gratuities to the judges' servants and bailiffs, £ 2, 15 s. for "sumthing for the judge," and about two-thirds of the total amount of £ 248, 19 s. 6 d. for food, drink, and lodging for men and horses.[31]

More than a century of parliamentary enactments and orders of the Council seem to have been of little or no avail in limiting these heavy expenses. Some of the country gentry, like Ffarington, tried single-handed to lessen the burden, and others, in groups, like thirty-five of the gentry of Northamptonshire, who, in an effort to enforce the statute of 1662 restricting the sheriff's expenses, drew up in 1676 elaborate rules to hold within more reasonable bounds the expenses of each of their number during his term.[32] Yet most of the sheriffs faced a deficit after their year in office, the expenses incurred in entertainment, together with the fees paid on entrance into and discharge from office, far exceeding their fees.

Administrative Work of the Assizes

After enjoying the banquets provided by their host the judges and the county magistrates took up the weightier matters of county administration. The

---

[30] *The Shrievalty of William Ffarington,* p. 17.
[31] *Somerset and Dorset Notes and Queries,* VII, 30.
[32] *Northamptonshire Notes and Queries,* I, 239-41.

high constables were often chosen at the Sheriff's Table, to take their oaths at the next quarter-sessions.[33] At one table treasurers were appointed to receive collections for the maimed soldiers within the county,[34] and at another an order passed for the giving in of the arrears of £300 imposed on the county for the relief of the poor. We also read of the justices coming to an agreement at the Sheriff's Table upon the price of corn in the county.[35]

Selection of a Chaplain

One part of the preparations for the assizes, the selection of a chaplain, remains to be described. We read that in 1621 the sheriff of Lancashire paid a certain Leigh forty shillings for speaking to the condemned prisoners at the summer assizes.[36] Ralph Josselin tells us in his diary of preaching the assize sermon and saying grace at the Sheriff's Table.[37] In all the instances noted the sheriff selected the chaplain for the assizes, though the church would seem to have had the better right. The political leanings of the person chosen had to be considered, for it was his duty to preach the assize sermon to the assembly; the members of the Privy Council for this reason, therefore, took notice of the appointments. A letter from the Council to the Archbishop of York, written in 1632, bewailed the type of person being

[33] Lancaster Sessions Rolls, April, 1650; *ibid.*, April, 1657.
[34] *Ibid.*, February, 1656-57.
[35] *Ibid.*, October, 1654. For printed references to the Sheriff's Board see *Manchester Sessions*, ed. Ernest Axon.
[36] Kenyon MSS, uncalendared.
[37] *Diary of the Rev. Ralph Josselin*, p. 34.

chosen for this office as being either unfriendly to
the present government, or lacking in "sufficiencie
or experience for those places and auditories (being
assemblies of the principall persons of each Countie),
and have given cause for scandal and offense which
is of dangerous consequence, and might bee easily
prevented, if election were made of discreete and
able men." The cause for the trouble was said to
lie in the choice of preachers by the sheriff without
leave of the bishop of the diocese. The Archbishop
was ordered to notify his bishops that the appointments in their dioceses either be made by them or
with their knowledge or approbation.[38]

[38] Historical Manuscripts Commission, *Report XIV*, Appendix, pt. IV, p. 49.

Chapter III

AS A CHANNEL OF GOVERNMENTAL COMMUNICATION

PUBLICATION OF PROCLAMATIONS

THE DUTIES of the sheriff as a channel of governmental communication represent his large usefulness both as the chief means of governmental communication within the county and as one of the strongest links holding the county government to the national government. Some of these duties were old; many were added by the Privy Council and Parliament during the period; as a group they distinguished the sheriff from the other royal officials in the county, though not so much as the holding of his county court or his entertaining at the assizes.

In reference to governmental communication within the county, the county-wide proclamation by the sheriff of quarter-sessions and the assizes has already been discussed. These courts informed the county through its head, the sheriff, of their administrative orders. For example, the Somerset quarter-sessions ordered the sheriff to proclaim the rates for wages made by the grand inquest for laborers, artificers, handicraftsmen, and others in open market in all cities and market towns within the county.[1] The quarter-sessions of the North Riding of York in 1655 ordered the sheriff to proclaim in all market towns the procedure to be followed by anyone ob-

[1] *Quarter-Sessions Records for the County of Somerset*, III, 263; also *North Riding of the County of York Quarter-Sessions Records*, VI, 5.

jecting to a marriage;² and in March, 1650/1 the Devon assizes commanded the under-sheriff to send copies of their order for the suppression of ale-houses to all corporations within the county.³ In these instances as in others of like nature the sheriff served as the regular channel of governmental communication within the county, a vital part of the machinery of county administration.

As the agent of the national government in the county the sheriff performed duties like the above in a much broader field. As the channel connecting the center with the parts he carried the orders of the state to the county and returned reports on the county to the state. Serving in this capacity the sheriff was responsible for the publication of all proclamations. Some statutes and many ordinances provided for their proclamation, often with the requirement that the sheriffs publish them "by sound of trumpet and beat of drum" at the next two county courts after their receipt, as well as in the usual places within the county and "in open market in the Shire Town."⁴

Election Responsibilities

Of all proclamations, the most widely published, excepting those of a new monarch, were notices of elections. Writs of election went forth out of the Chancery to the sheriffs directing them to command the county to choose its knights, and to require each city and town which had the right, to choose its

² *Ibid.*, V, 197.
³ Assizes, 24/21, Order Book, 1641-52.
⁴ *Acts and Ordinances of the Interregnum*, I, 1019; II, 354.

citizens or burgesses. In his next county court after receipt of the writ the sheriff proclaimed the day and place of the new Parliament, and then in the full county supervised the election. The names of the two successful knights *"gladiis cinctos"* were inserted in an indenture, or certificate of election, made between the sheriff and the voters, and returned by the sheriff with the writ to the Chancery by the day set for the opening of Parliament.[5] This constituted the sheriff's return. The sheriff also, after receipt of the writ, sent warrants under his seal to the head officials of the cities and boroughs within his county, reciting the writ and commanding them to choose their representations to Parliament, and then to return to him indentures of their elections. A fourteenth-century statute embodied in the *nolumus* clause of the writ of election forbade the sheriff's returning himself or another sheriff, but this restriction was not always observed during the struggle between King and Parliament.[6] No person could take his seat in the House of Commons until the sheriff had made return of his writ to the Clerk of the Crown in Chancery.

[5] An indenture of the election of 1656 is to be found in William Hutchinson's *The History and Antiquities of the County Palatine of Durham*, I, 530 n.

[6] An interesting discussion of this point is to be found in Professor Harold Hulme's article, "The Sheriff as a Member of the House of Commons from Elizabeth to Cromwell," *Journal of Modern History*, Vol. I (September, 1929). Copies of writs of election are given in *Journals of the House of Commons*, I, 140, and in *Acts and Ordinances of the Interregnum*, II, 1469-72.

Election days were undoubtedly an exciting time for the county, the county court being aroused for the time being out of its characteristic dullness as a judicial body into a very lively and, all too often, a very disorderly assembly. While the presence of the sheriff at the ordinary monthly courts seems to have been infrequent, either the under-sheriff or county clerk taking his place, the responsibilities of supervision, the return of elections, and, it must be said of some of the sheriffs, the splendid opportunities presented for the use of personal influence and of corrupt manipulation, drew him to court at this season.[7] When one considers the frequency with which sheriffs appeared on bended knee before the bar of the House of Commons to crave its pardon, and the large number who were fined or imprisoned in the Tower for interfering with the freedom of elections, it is clear that many took great liberties with their election responsibilities.[8] The most common charges against the sheriff were: that he had removed the place of election to another part of the county most favorable to the choice of his candidates; that he had permitted to vote those not qualified; that he had closed the polls while his friends were in the lead; and that he had pronounced and returned elected those not elected.[9]

[7] The sheriff of Huntingdon and Cambridge needed the help of his assistants for those two counties and the Isle of Ely.—*Calendar of State Papers, Domestic, 1654*, p. 208.

[8] *Journals of the House of Commons*, I, 739; *The Journal of Sir Simonds D'Ewes*, pp. 110 n., 302.

[9] *Diary of Henry Townshend of Elmley Lovett, 1640-1663*, I, 19; *The Journal of Sir Simonds D'Ewes*, p. 95; *Autobiography of Sir John Bramston*, pp. 162, 377.

Election Worries

On the other hand, county court elections had some vexations and risks for the sheriff. D'Ewes, who was sheriff of Suffolk in 1640, upon receipt of a writ for an election to the Long Parliament, notified the bailiffs and others of Dunwich that when they appeared in his next county court to hear the reading of the proclamation of election he would give them their warrant authorizing the election for Dunwich. This he stated was for his own protection, since at the previous election[10] he had been in danger of a fine for the reason that some of his warrants, which he had left signed and sealed at Ipswich to be carefully sent from there to some of the boroughs of the county, had, quite contrary to his intentions, been detained, and as a result the indentures of their elections, to be sent in with the county indenture and the writ, were returned to him only two days before the beginning of Parliament. He asked them to make their choice "with all convenient speede" and send their indenture either to him or to the Clerk of the Crown.[11]

In this letter D'Ewes speaks of the "taxes and troubles of my Shreivaltie in this yeare past." The election for the Short Parliament must have worried him greatly, for added to the anxiety of getting his returns in on time was that of securing a free election for the county. As previously remarked, one finds here and there in the records complaints against

[10] To the Short Parliament, meeting April 13, 1640.
[11] Harleian MSS, CLXV, 11-12.

the sheriff for adjourning his court to a part of the county most favorable to his candidates because so difficult of access to the supporters of the opposition;[12] but D'Ewes describes in some detail how he thwarted the evil designs of certain persons who conspired to hinder a free election and thereby ruin his reputation, by secretly contriving the adjournment of the county court from its usual place of meeting to a distant and less accessible part of the county.[13]

As General Intermediary

While serving as an active go-between for such purposes as the publishing of orders and proclamations, and the supervising and reporting of elections, the sheriff at other times was little more than an intermediary between the central and local governments. In the 1630's, when the state was particularly active in supervising county administration, he was constantly being required to furnish the Council directly, or indirectly through the judges on circuit, information on the state of the county gathered by the justices of the peace. In one instance the justices reported to the sheriff of Essex their execution of the directions of the Council relative to the sale and the price of corn, that after taking account of what corn every grower had in his barns, of the number of persons in his family, and of the number of acres to be sown, they had allotted the amount each person should carry to market weekly.[14] The justices of

[12] Historical Manuscripts Commission, *Report XIII*, Appendix, pt. I, pp. 318-19.
[13] Harleian MSS, CLX, 151-52.
[14] *Calendar of State Papers, Domestic, 1629-31*, p. 415

Warwickshire in 1631 reported to the sheriff their proceedings for relief of the poor to the effect that the fewness of the ale-houses, "the true nurseries of almost all the disorders pointed at in the Book of Orders," gave them little to certify;[15] those of Leicester sent to the sheriff a certificate of presentments made before them concerning the punishment of rogues and vagabonds within one of the hundreds.[16] The justices sent to the sheriff lists of those who had apprentices, those who kept ale-houses, the number of apprentices bound, the number of ale-houses suppressed, and the number of vagrants punished.[17] All this information the sheriff forwarded to the Council.[18] In certain instances he reveals even more clearly his usefulness to the state. For example, Richard Bold, sheriff of Lancashire, reported to the Council that he had received from the preceding sheriff their letter concerning the prevention of the dearth of corn; that he had published the proclamation and Book of Orders at the last quarter-sessions and after the assizes would give in an account of the proceedings of the justices and of the state of the county.[19]

As Temporary Treasurer

As the chief means of communication the sheriff was often called upon to act as a temporary treasurer

[15] *Ibid., 1631-33*, pp. 133-34.
[16] *Ibid.*, p. 169.
[17] *Ibid., 1633-34*, p. 408; *ibid., 1634-35*, p. 106.
[18] *Calendar of State Papers, Domestic, 1629-31*, pp. 420, 525, etc.
[19] *Ibid.*, p. 505; see also pp. 406, 543, 550.

or receive. In 1648 the House of Commons ordered all contributions made throughout England and Wales for the wounded soldiers and the "poor visited people" of Lancashire to be paid to the sheriffs, who, in turn, were to send on the money to certain designated persons for distribution.[20] At an earlier date, 1621, the justices of Lancashire, gathered around the Sheriff's Table during the summer assizes, ordered the high sheriff to pay over to a committee of their number the money contributed for the repair of a bridge in the county, and the committee to report at the Table during the next summer assizes regarding the disbursement of the money.[21] In addition to these duties as temporary county treasurer, the sheriff was often designated to receive from collectors the sums of money voted by Parliament and to pay over the same to a permanent treasurer.[22]

[20] Partington MSS, Military Annals of Lancaster, p. 102; see also *Acts and Ordinances of the Interregnum,* I, 1003.
[21] *Manchester Sessions,* I, 151.
[22] *Journals of the House of Commons,* II, 269, 290; VIII, 298; 16 Car. I, c. 30 and c. 33; 12 Car. II, c. 9, etc.

Chapter IV

THE SHERIFF'S COUNTY COURT

Importance of the County Court

THE HOLDING of the county court was one of the oldest of the sheriff's duties. While this must have been an important part of his work in the early days of the office when the county court had much administrative and judicial business, a continued narrowing of its sphere of activity resulted from the increasing supervision of the royal courts over county affairs and the extension of their jurisdictions. The judicial interpretation of the statute of Gloucester of 1278 had limited its jurisdiction over debt and other personal actions to causes where the amount involved was under forty shillings, unless the writ of *Justicies* were purchased authorizing the sheriff to preside over suits for greater amounts. Legal historians have not yet made a thorough study of the county court in the seventeenth century as a judicial body; this may be because they conceive of it at that time as a mediaeval survival, of little value to the community. The entire absence of county court records[1] makes such a study exceedingly difficult, for indirect sources can give us at best only an incom-

---

[1] The discovery within recent years of a few plea rolls of county courts held during the reigns of Edward III and Richard II explodes the old theory that the court kept no written records. See article by H. Jenkinson, "Plea Rolls of the Mediaeval County Courts," *Cambridge Historical Journal*, 1923, I, pt. I. Because of this discovery there is less reason to conclude that written records were not kept by the court in the seventeenth century, though they have not yet been found.

plete picture of the court, of its officials, of the suitors, and of court business and procedure. Yet such information as we derive from the records, however small, is bound to be well worth our attention in this study of the development of colonial institutions out of their English origins; for undoubtedly the emigrants to Virginia and Maryland in the seventeenth century were familiar with the county court and made use of their knowledge of it in working out their judicial systems. The place of the English county court in the development of colonial judiciary belongs, however, to a later chapter on the colonial courts.

The Middleton Case

A bill of complaint of Christopher Middleton of the county of Leicester to the Court of Star Chamber,[2] together with the account of several suits brought from the county court of the Palatinate of Durham to the Durham Court of Pleas on writs of false judgment, contain valuable information concerning the nature of county court proceedings in England during the first half of the seventeenth century. In the first document, dated 1610, Middleton claimed that he had had lawful possession of a certain piece of land in W., until R. M., T. K., H. W., and others entered his land and disseised him of a horse and cow. He went to the under-sheriff's deputy and entered a plaint of replevin against the three, and the deputy thereupon replevied and delivered his cattle to him. At the next county court meeting in

[2] Star Chamber Proceedings, James I, bundle 209, file 21.

THE SHERIFF'S COUNTY COURT

May at the Castle of Leicester, at which he and the three defendants appeared, he entered his declaration against them for the unjust taking of his cattle against securities. They impleaded to the declaration until the next county court.³ At the court held on June 21 the defendants traversed the taking of the cattle on Middleton's land, as alleged by the plaintiff, and avowed taking the cattle at H. as bailiffs to Sir Henry Skipworth, because they were damaging his freehold there. Middleton was then given day until the next Court to plead in bar to the avowry.

At the sessions of July 19 the attorney for the defendants, Robert Pilkington, having died since the last Court, "yt was then and there moved by Sr Henry Hastings knight a good ffreeholder of the said Countie, and beinge then and yet one of his Ma^{ts} deputie lieftenaunts of the said Countie of Leicester and one of his Ma^{ts} Justice of peace for the same Countie, and by others that further day might be given for all such cawses as the said Robert Pilkington was toward wch was graunted by the then Courte and the attorney of the said Middleton praied then & there further day for the reasons aforesaid." Yet notwithstanding all this, the complainant continues,

³ In an action of replevin the complainant had to give the sheriff bond to prosecute his action at the next county court before the property disseised would be restored to him. The Kenyon Manuscripts at Gredington Hall, uncalendared, contain bonds for £10, £20, and £40, dated 1628, and made to the sheriff for recovery of two kine, four kine, and a mare and colt respectively. For the law of replevin, see Greenwood, *County Court* (3rd ed., 1668), pp. 34-38.

the under-sheriff, without rule or warrant of the court, entered a judgment against him of *nihil dicit* and awarded one writ to inquire of the damages for the defendants against the plaintiff, and another to return the cattle to the defendants. At the court of August 16 the sheriff's bailiff returned twelve men to inquire of the damages. They were sworn by the under-sheriff, who then, though without warrant of the court, told the jury that they ought to find some damages for the defendants, although claim was made by Middleton's attorney that the action had been stayed by the court, and furthermore that no evidence had been given the jury to prove the defendants damaged by the *nihil dicit* of the plaintiff. Yet despite the argument of his counsel, Middleton complains, the under-sheriff directed the jury to find damages for the defendants, and they, being bribed, gave a verdict for 3 s. 4 d. Thereupon, the under-sheriff, without any warrant or direction from the county court, gave judgment for the recovery of 3 s. 4 d. and for costs 18 s. 2 d.; and without warrant of the court ordered the bailiff to levy damages and costs on his goods, and to return the cattle to the defendants. The plaintiff sums up his complaint with the charge that the jurors had maliciously given a false verdict; that the under-sheriff, though not judge, and without warrant of the suitors who were the judges, gave days to the defendants to answer and to the plaintiff to reply; that he gave judgment against the plaintiff and awarded a writ of inquiry and return; that he gave direction to the jury without warrant of court and contrary to law, and gave judgment on their verdict and awarded execution: all without warrant of the suitors, who alone were the judges of the court.

In answer to this bill of complaint the *jurors admit this account of the proceedings to be true* but deny having been bribed. As for the authority of the under-sheriff they say that he or his deputy "time out of memorye of man . . . ever directed all proceedings and the iuryes upon all maner of trials." Their defense is, therefore, that they had simply carried out the directions of the under-sheriff, who had always directed proceedings in the county court.

Court Membership and Procedure

Here we see the county court meeting at the Castle of Leicester every four weeks for at least three consecutive months. The meetings might be held in any town in the county at the pleasure of the sheriff except in those counties whose place of meeting was determined by statute.[4] The court was convened during this period every lunar month in the Castle or in the shire hall.[5] The practice of holding the county court every twenty-eight days as prescribed by statute[6] was continued in Lancashire as late as the nineteenth century.[7]

[4] Dalton, *Officium Vicecomitum,* cap. 109.
[5] Greenwood, *Curia Comitatus Rediviva* (1657), pp. 63-64; Kenyon MSS, uncalendared (Lancashire, 1628); Lancaster Sessions Rolls, January, 1641-42; April, 1656; July, 1657, etc.; Star Chamber Proceedings, James I, bundle 217, file 16 (Lincolnshire, 1610); *The Cheshire Sheaf,* III, 116-17.
[6] 2 & 3 Ed. VI, c. 25.
[7] *Second and Final Report of the Commissioners Appointed to Inquire into the Course of Proceedings in Suits, &c. in the Courts of the County Palatine of Lancaster, 1836.*

Attending the trial of "the Middleton case" were the deputy sheriff, his bailiff, counsel for the parties to the suit, a deputy lieutenant who was also a knight and justice of the peace, other suitors, and a jury of twelve men. Of these the activities of the deputy lieutenant and the other suitors and their relations with each other are most obscure. The participation of the body of suitors in the court proceedings is worth noting because this signifies the survival of the ancient communal organization of the county court down to the modern era. But by what method did the suitors reach agreement on questions before them? Did the more influential suitors guide the judgments of the body, as is suggested by the action of Hastings and "others" present? Unfortunately the records give us only this one glimpse of the suitors arriving at a decision in the more simple matter of adjournment, when Sir Henry Hastings and "others" moved to adjourn the case, and their motion was granted by the court. Another case was said to have been tried before four of the suitors instead of before the sheriff, although as chairmen they could not legally act as judges.[8] If we may borrow evidence from the early nineteenth century, a parliamentary commission reported that while in the county court of the County Palatine of Lancaster the suitors were still the judges by law, in practice the sheriff retained two barristers as judges.[9] This

[8] Durham Judgment Rolls, 13/36, *rot.* 19-20.
[9] *Second and Final Report of the Commissioners Appointed to Inquire into . . . the Courts of the County Palatine of Lancaster, 1836.*

evidence, though slight, indicates a probability that in the seventeenth century a few of the suitors, more learned in the law or more influential in the county, advised and directed the rest in the court proceedings.[10]

BIGLAND VS. LANGDALE

Then, too, there is the question to be answered of the proper place of the sheriff in the county court. Lacking as we do the decrees and orders of the Court of Star Chamber,[11] we cannot from this case know whether the under-sheriff had, or had not, by his actions exceeded his authority, as the complainant contended. But the opinion of the judges in Beecher's case, delivered two years before, had been that the suitors are the judges.[12] That the suitors and not the under-sheriff rightfully acted as the judges may be seen in the records of the following suits brought up to the Court of Pleas at Durham from the county court on writs of false judgment. The sheriff in each case is ordered by the judges to have a record made in the full county court[13] of the plea now before the judges but previously in the county court, and to have that record at a certain date before them, under his seal and the seals of four legal knights of those who were present at the record. The

[10] Professor W. A. Morris of the University of California discusses this vital matter in reference to the 13th century county court in his valuable work, *The Early English County Court*, pp. 106 ff.
[11] Giuseppi, *A Guide to the Manuscripts Preserved in the Public Record Office*, I, 272.
[12] Exchequer: 6 Jas. I, 8 Co. Rep., 60.—*Coke's Reports*.
[13] *In pleno comitatu.*

record in the suit of *Bigland* vs. *Langdale* stated that B. had complained in the county court of Durham[14] against L. in a plea of trespass upon the case on assumpsit to his damage of £ 10.[15] In his declaration at the next county court B. made the same complaint against L. but at this time to his damage of £ 12. By his attorney he pleaded that in a late suit of debt in the county court of *Crosby* vs. *Danby*, L. had requested the bailiff to permit the defendant to go at large, which the bailiff granted, after B., at L.'s solicitation and promise of security, had become pledged for him. As a result, B. complained, of L.'s failure to keep his promise, he had been damaged to the value of £ 12, and had thereupon produced suit. L., then, through his attorney, petitioned an imparlance[16] to the twentieth of July (1612), and at that court again to the seventeenth of August. On the seventeenth of August, L., appearing by his attorney, defended the force and injury, to the effect that he had not promised in the manner and form of B.'s complaint; he thereupon put himself upon the country. B. did likewise, and, issue being joined, the bailiff was commanded *venire faceret coram prefato vicecomite ad comitatum suum tunc tentum eodem XVIj° die augusti duodecim etc. per quos etc. ad inquirendum, etc.* The twelve men duly assembled by the bailiff *super sacramentum* stated the fact: that L. had assumed upon himself and promised as B. had

---

[14] *In curia comitatus Dunelm'*.
[15] Durham Judgment Rolls, 13/15, *rot*. 2-2d.
[16] *Petiit licenciam inde interloquendi*.

previously declared against him, and they gave a judgment for damages and costs to B., by reason of the promise unfulfilled, of £ 10, 13 s., 1 d. The court thereupon decided[17] that B. should recover against L. this amount, and that L. be in mercy.

In answer to this record L. declared before the judges that false judgment had been given him in the county court in diverse ways. In the first place, while B. in said plea stated his damages to have been £ 10, in the declaration it was £ 12; which statements were contradictory, and so there was no judgment returned upon said plea. Secondly, the sheriff had not received a writ of *Justicies* from the Chancery of Durham authorizing him to hold this plea in his county court. Because of these and other defects in the record L. petitioned the annulling of the judgment.

The record of this interesting suit ends with the statement that these things being heard and diligently inquired into, it seemed to the judges that in various ways L. had been given false judgment, and therefore because of said defects in the record and others it was decided that the judgment was false and consequently revoked; L. was to be restored all things which through false judgment he had lost, and the *suitors of the county court of Durham were in mercy.*[18]

[17] *Ideo consideratum est per curiam.*
[18] *Et sectatores predicte curie comitatus Dunelm' in misericordia,* etc.

The Sheriff as Chairman and Executive

In this account the exclusively judicial functions of the suitors is the striking fact. In the first case the under-sheriff, after the finding of damages by the jury, gave the judgment; in the second the court gave judgment for the damages and cost found by the jury. In another suit in the county court of Durham we see the court giving judgment for the plaintiff on failure of answer by the defendant, and the sheriff ordering his bailiff to take the defendant into custody until he paid the costs.[19] In the Middleton case, it will be remembered, the under-sheriff gave judgment for the defendant on a *nihil dicit*. But the most conclusive evidence to show that judgments in the county court of the seventeenth century still belonged rightfully to the suitors and not to the sheriff, under-sheriff, or county clerk is the statement in the above case of the amercement of the suitors for false judgment.

Suits were begun in the county court in one of two ways, by plaint or by writ. If the action involved an amount below forty shillings it was begun by a complaint and, according to Dalton, might be tried by compurgation.[20] We have an example of a trial by jury of a case involving 39 s. 11 d., instituted without writ,[21] but none of compurgation. Is it not probable that compurgation at this late date was almost abandoned and that trial by jury had taken

---

[19] Durham Judgment Rolls, 13/36, *rot.* 19.
[20] *Officium Vicecomitum,* cap. 110.
[21] Durham Judgment Rolls, 13/26, *rot.* 18-18d.

its place as the usual method of proof? Were compurgation used then the court would be nearer its original self. The trial of suits to the amount of forty shillings and above was authorized by the writ of *Justicies*. With the writ, of course, went the use of a jury of fact. Contemporary writers, however, are agreed that the nature of the court was not altered by the use of these parts of the King's judicial machinery, but that the suitors remained the judges, and the sheriff the presiding official. The seventeenth-century county court in its organization, with the sheriff as presiding official and the suitors as judges, seems a perpetuation of its early communal organization; but its pleadings and its means of getting at the truth through a jury of fact make its procedure that of a common law court.

The two cases just analysed supplemented by others also give some conception, even though vague, of the sheriff's true place in the county court.[22] The county court was, in the broadest sense, the sheriff's court.[23] Defendants were attached to appear before the sheriff at his next county court, and the defendant was "convict before the sheriff in the county."[24] The sheriff appointed the officials of the court: the under-sheriff, county clerk,[25] and bailiff

[22] No distinction can be made between the high sheriff and his under-sheriff in regard to their court duties; only in regard to their rights in the county court.

[23] Jentleman's case, King's Bench, 25 Eliz., *6 Co. Rep.*, 11a-12b.—*Coke's Reports.*

[24] Beecher's case, Exchequer, 6 Jas. I, *8 Co. Rep.*, 60b.—*Coke's Reports.*

[25] Mitton's case, King's Bench, 26 Eliz., *4 Co. Rep.*, 32b-34b.—*Coke's Reports.*

—all except the coroners, who were elected by the freeholders there assembled.[26] Furthermore, the sheriff, or usually his under-sheriff for the sheriff was not often present, to some extent organized the court: he took security to prosecute there in actions of replevin,[27] and he forced defendants to appear either by taking them into custody[28] or by attaching their property.[29] We have also noted the under-sheriff impanelling and swearing the jury.[30]

But the sheriff was principally the court executive, as illustrated by the following record: G. R. complained against M. M. in a plea of debt of 32 s. 7 d. in the county court, and M. M. making no defense it was decided by the court that G. R. should recover his debt and damages against M. M., and that M. M. be in mercy. Afterwards the sheriff directed his bailiff to take M. M. in custody until he paid the amount. The bailiff returning the defendant not found, the plaintiff prayed the sheriff his remedy against M. L. as pledge for M. M., and the sheriff directed his writ to the bailiff that *scire facias prefato Matheo Liddell Manucaptori predicto quod sit coram me prefato Vicecomite ad proximum comitatum meum apud Dunelm' tenendum die lune dec-*

[26] The coroners had the important duty of declaring outlawry in the court, see Rev. J. C. Cox's *Three Centuries of Derbyshire Annals*, I, 88-89.
[27] Kenyon MSS, uncalendared.
[28] Durham Judgment Rolls, 13/36, *rot*. 19.
[29] Lancaster Sessions Rolls, 1641, 1653.
[30] Star Chamber Proceedings, James I, 209/21. The county clerk at times performed this duty and also at times presided over the court.—Star Chamber Proceedings, James I, 217/16.

imo die Februarij proximi to answer why G. R. should not recover his debt from him. Later in the proceedings, M. L. as pledge making no defense, it was decided by the court that G. R. should recover against M. L. his debt and damages and M. L. be in mercy. So the sheriff directed another writ to his bailiff commanding him to have M. L. appear before him at his next court to show cause why G. R. should not have his debt and damages.[31]

This account completes our knowledge of the sheriff's activities in the county court by showing him executing its judgments through his bailiff. However, from this and the other cases cited we see clearly that he was more than the court's servant organizing the court and executing its judgments as at quarter-sessions and the assizes, for he presided over the county court, pronounced the judgments of the suitors, and had definite rights of the court incident to the office of sheriff.

JURISDICTION OF THE COUNTY COURT

Greenwood tells us that in this period the county court held plea of the smaller personal actions under forty shillings by way of plaint, those of debt, replevin, detinue, trespass, trover and conversion, etc., and of forty shillings and above by writ of *Justicies*.[32] Suits in the county court are mentioned where the amounts involved ranged all the way from nineteen shillings to seventy pounds. The fairly frequent recording of suits far above forty shillings in

[31] Durham Judgment Rolls, 13/16, *rot.* 19-20.
[32] Greenwood, *County Court* (1668), pp. 12-13, 39.

amount causes wonder as to whether the county court was as unimportant and little used in this period as is commonly supposed.

The jurisdiction of the court was important enough to merit the attention of one law reformer who, writing in 1621 under the title, "matters needed to be Reformed in Course of Law," proposed that writs of *Justicies* in county courts be limited to debts not exceeding five pounds, "for only the undersheriff or clerk of the court sits there, who, for the most parte, hath no judgment to determine in greater causes."[33] At a later date, 1639 (?), 115 of the gentry of Cheshire certified that by reason of the grants of writs of *Justicies* out of the Chester Court of Exchequer, the inhabitants of the said county had "enjoyed great ease and benefit, for that upon these writs there was quick proceeding; and debts there recovered in shorter time and at less charge than in any other court within that county."[34] It would be interesting to know how the Cheshire County court was conducted at this date to make it a more useful court than the other county courts seem to have been.

Defects of the County Court

However unsatisfactory this evidence may seem in assisting one to measure the activity of the county court at this date, there is, on the other hand, important evidence of certain defects in the county court which would be bound to limit its usefulness to litigants. A fifteenth-century statute had provided that

[33] *Rutland MSS*, IV, 215.
[34] *Calendar of State Papers, Domestic, 1639-40*, p. 249.

THE SHERIFF'S COUNTY COURT 51

two justices view the sheriff's entries of plaints in the county court and also his estreats of amercements,[35] and there is frequent mention in the quarter-sessions records of the justices of the peace appointing certain of their number to execute this law.[36] Yet complaints came up to the Court of Star Chamber of either the under-sheriff or the county clerk entering false complaints[37] and making false amercements, even to the extent of substituting false lists of shire amercements for those already signed by the justices of the peace.[38] These complaints, with others, of the under-sheriff's suborning the jury[39] and trespassing on the privileges of the suitors, do not prove the county court to be corrupt at this time, but suggest rather the good opportunities for corruption permitted the chief officials of the court, the under-sheriff and the county clerk in their capacities as its executive and secretarial officers. The probable reason for the proposed law reform in 1621 was the need to restrict the jurisdiction of the under-sheriff and county clerk to smaller suits, where the injury they might work would be less.

In addition to the under-sheriff and the county clerk, the sheriff's bailiffs, as might be expected from what we have already learned of them, were also

[35] 11 Henry VII, c. 15. See also Dalton, *The Countrey Justice*, c. 90.
[36] *Quarter-Sessions Records for the County of Somerset*, II, 57, 58, 265; III, 106, 139, 164, 234; *North Riding of the County of York Quarter-Sessions Records*, VII, 3, 7.
[37] Star Chamber Proceedings, James I, 304/32.
[38] *Ibid.*, 118/19.
[39] *Ibid.*, 54/15; 15/26.

found dishonest in the performance of their county court duties. Greenwood saw in them the cause for the court's being in disgrace, in that the ignorant people were much abused and deceived by "those Locusts . . . irreligious Harpies, scraping, griping Catch-poles, Bayliffs" who are the sole causes of "those ignominious aspersions cast upon the Court." It would be a great advantage to the Commonwealth, he thought, if the statute of Henry V, c. 4 were observed and the sheriff's bailiffs not again allowed in office until three years afterwards, because by their continued being in office they grow "so crafty and cunning, that they are able to deceive the sheriff, and ruine the whole Country."[40]

Again, these documents show the procedure in the county court to have been very slow as well as complicated. There were the almost unending adjournments of suits from one court to another, presumably to give one party more time to answer the pleadings of the other. But to what extent, if any, the superior courts excelled the county court in the particulars of speedier and more certain justice and of less expense to the suitor, is a large and difficult study and beyond the scope of this essay.

We have attempted nothing more than to present some evidence regarding the nature of the sheriff's county court—its organization, jurisdiction, procedure and seeming defects—within the period when the colonists were drawing upon their knowledge of English local institutions for the building of their own county governments.

[40] Greenwood, *County Court* (1668), p. 26.

Chapter V
FINANCIAL DUTIES
Collector of Prerogative Revenues

From the earliest date the sheriff had been the King's bailiff to conserve and collect the royal rights and revenues in the county. The traditional revenues of the King, which he possessed independently of Parliament, were derived from many sources: feudal rights, rents, fines, forfeitures of the goods of felons and of outlaws, deodands, wreck of the sea, waifs and estrays, treasure trove,[1] whales, wild swans, and from various other casualties too numerous to mention.[2] Twice a year these items were listed in the Summons of the Pipe sent down by the Exchequer to the sheriffs, who rendered their accounts at Easter and Michaelmas at the Exchequer. Most of these revenues were mere survivals of an early age and generally insignificant. Some were half-forgotten or non-existent; others were scattered, and not only expensive but difficult to collect.[3]

King vs. Parliament

These ancient financial obligations of the sheriff to the King were, during the period 1603-40, greatly increased through the efforts of James I and Charles

[1] An interesting example of treasure trove is to be found in the *Calendar of State Papers, Domestic, 1661-62*, p. 533.
[2] Dalton, *Officium Vicecomitum*, caps. 5, 7, and 9.
[3] Sir Matthew Hale, *A Short Treatise Touching Sheriff's Accompts*, pp. 68-69. Hale commented on the insignificance in his day of the profits of the sheriff's courts, the county court, and his "tourn and leet."

I to become financially independent of Parliament.[4] Could the Stuarts secure sufficient revenues for their needs without recourse to Parliament they might rule with unlimited power—their object in view. The personal revenues of the Crown being found quite inadequate to this end, they vastly augmented these incomes by the collection of various extra-parliamentary revenues for which were found good precedents and almost unanimous judicial support.

The Council expected all the royal officials in the county to assist in the collection of the extraordinary revenues, but the chief responsibility seems to have been delegated to the justices of the peace and the sheriff. These officials are to be found closely coöperating in the collection of benevolences, forced loans, compositions for knighthood, and ship-money.

Benevolences

James sought benevolences on three different occasions, in 1614-15, 1620, and 1622. In an effort to recover "the patrimony of his children in Germany," he commanded, in 1622, the justices and sheriff of each county, after grouping themselves into committees, to call before them one by one, and take the subscriptions of, the principal men of the county. They were to appoint collectors to receive the contributions and return with the money a list of those who gave

[4] Feudal aids had not been collected by the rulers of England for more than a century before 1609, when Prince Henry the eldest son of James I, was knighted, and 1612, when Princess Elizabeth married.

and those who refused to give. Thus could James, characteristically, distinguish his enemies from his friends in each county. The royal officials themselves were expected to give liberally. In Devonshire twenty-six of the justices and the sheriff subscribed at quarter-sessions a total of £ 233, 10 s., and the sheriff led all the others with a gift of £ 40.[5] The greater part of the work of assembling prospective subscribers before the justices, of collecting their pledged contributions, and of returning to the justices or sheriff lists of those who had paid and of those delinquent was performed by the constables of the hundreds. The money was turned over to the sheriff; the lists of givers, of non-givers, and excuses for the smallness of the benevolence were forwarded to the Council either by the sheriff or by the justices.[6]

Forced Loans and Compositions for Knighthood

Much the same system was employed in collecting the forced loan of 1626 and compositions for knighthood in 1630. Commissioners for the Loan were appointed for each county of the chief county officials, who, acting in the capacity of supervisors, reported to the Council their proceedings and the names of those who had loaned to the King and those who had refused. The loans were paid into the Exchequer by the sheriff or by one of the justices ap-

[5] Hamilton, *Quarter-Sessions from Queen Elizabeth to Queen Anne,* pp. 52-54, 65.
[6] *Ibid.,* pp. 50-51; *Calendar of State Papers, Domestic, 1619-23,* pp. 388, 398, 408.

pointed as collector.[7] Commissions of county officials were likewise appointed for receiving compositions from those with an annual income of £ 40 refusing to accept knighthood. One member of the commission was appointed collector. They were directed to find out from the sheriff, the escheator, constables, and from various property lists obtainable, what persons in the county were subject to fines for their estates. They were to take into account whatever part of the compositions had already been returned by the sheriff, and to fine those in the commission of the peace not less than £ 26, "it being presumed that they are all of good estates answerable thereto." From fines, as from benevolences, a disproportionate part of the wealth of the principal county officials was exacted in addition to their services to the King in rating and collecting.[8]

Collection of Ship-Money

As for the collection of ship-money during the years 1634 to 1640 the Council imposed the chief responsibility on the sheriff. His procedure in assessing and collecting the amount demanded in the writ gives us our best picture of the royal system of collection as distinguished from that employed by Parliament for the collection of its grants. Humphrey Chetham, sheriff of Lancashire in 1635, first called a meeting of the mayors and burgesses to as-

[7] *Ibid., 1625-26,* p. 165; *ibid., 1627-28,* pp. 273, 332, 336.
[8] *Lancashire and Cheshire Record Society Publications,* XII, 199-223; *Calendar of State Papers, Domestic, 1629-31,* pp. 283, 356.

FINANCIAL DUTIES

sess the towns in his county. He then divided the remainder of the sum demanded among the hundreds of the county and sent his warrants to the high constables of each hundred to assess, with the help of the petty constables and the more influential men of the hundred, the amount on each parish and village of the hundred. The assessments were returned to the sheriff under the signatures of the high constables; he examined the lists and sent out warrants under the seal of his office to the high constables to collect and to pay in the money to him at Preston within forty days. Though the second assessment of ship-money was better received by the people than those following, it was answered by loud complaints of unfair division, especially from the clergy and the poor. When Chetham reached Preston at the appointed time with a guard to receive the allotted £ 3,500 and convey it to his house, he found the town in a tumult and very little ship-money collected. The high constables excused themselves by putting the blame on those next below them in rank, the petty constables; and these officials, being last in line of the collectors and so unable to follow suit, could only protest to the sheriff that though they had done their very best to collect, many persons could not pay, others they had had to distrain, and still others on whom they had tried to distrain they could find no property to levy upon. The constables, high and petty, might offer excuses to the sheriff but the sheriff could not excuse himself to the Council. He was made personally responsible for the collection.⁹ Chetham then took charge, settled the assessment himself, and got the money collected and sent to the Treasurer of the Navy before the year was out.¹⁰ The cost of collecting the £ 3,500 amounted to £ 96.¹¹

General Deductions

From the description of the system employed in the collection of ship-money and the other extra-parliamentary revenues certain principles may be deduced. In the first place, the assessors, collectors, and receivers were county officials who had been appointed directly or indirectly by the Crown, to execute not these particular duties alone but a large variety of other duties as well; grants made by Parliament, on the other hand, were collected by commissioners appointed either by Parliament or by the great officers of the Crown, according to the nature of the grant, for the performance of that particular

[9] S. R. Gardiner, *History of England from 1603 to 1642*, VIII, 93, 102.

[10] Chetham MSS and Memoirs, V, 37.

[11] *Ibid.*, p. 49. Some of the more interesting items follow:

"At the first convention of the Mayor Burgesses & Bailiffs of the Corporate and Borough Towns for the Assessing of ye townes . . . £1. 3s. 10d.

"For sev[ll]. Warrants sent out at severall tymes to the High Constables of the Hundreds of the Co. both for making their assessm[ts] & other meetings to view the same and for the Collecting of the Money Assessed . . . £1. 13s. 0d.

"Spent by the charge of 16 men and 20 horses in our Journey to Preston in one week for receaving and bringing home of 2000 [li] received of 4 of the Hundreds of the Co. and in payment thereof to the Exchangers . . . £23. 18s. 10d.

"To the High Constables for such Charges as they disbursed out of Purse and travell some 180 miles some 140 and some 80 miles & in collecting & car[y] their money to Preston . . . £15. 3s. 10d."

duty. Parliament, quite probably, was too jealous of the royal power to trust the King's local officials with work involving so much responsibility. Secondly, the hundred and not the county was clearly the unit of assessment and collection. Whatever original powers the hundred had lost by the Stuart period it was still constantly being used for purposes of taxation, as for military levy and equipment, and conservation of the peace.[12] Finally, the increasing dependence placed by the Stuarts in the period 1603-40 on their own revenues, and in particular the regular collection of ship-money between 1634 and 1640, added greatly to the sheriff's duties for the time being and to his power and influence in the county. His most responsible duties in the years when James I and Charles I were anxiously seeking independent incomes were not as executive official of the courts, as contemporary writers suggest, but as collector and receiver for the King of the extra-parliamentary revenues in each county. In the Chesapeake colonies the power of the sheriff in local government, as we will observe, was due principally to his employment by the King and the colony in the collection of royal and colonial revenues.

[12] E. P. Cheyney, *A History of England from the Defeat of the Armada to the Death of Elizabeth*, II, 389.

PART II
THE SHERIFF IN THE CHESAPEAKE COLONIES

Chapter VI
QUALIFICATIONS AND APPOINTMENT
Early Conditions in Virginia

THE FIRST period in the institutional history of Virginia, from the year of the first settlement in 1607 until the colony became self-governing in 1619, was characterized by unsettled economic and political conditions. The population was small, consisting by 1619 of no more than six hundred settlers, scattered along the James River and engaged, for most of the period, in a struggle with the environment for their very existence. During these early years of hardships and dangers the colony was governed arbitrarily, from 1607 to 1609, by the King and by the President and Council in Virginia, and, during the years following, under the Divine, Moral, and Martial laws imposed by the governors Gates, Dale, and Argoll. There was but one court, the General Court, composed at first of the President and the Council, which had been invested originally with full political and judicial powers. However, its decisions were given, not as directed by charter, in accordance with the laws of England, but as dictated by the personal animosities of its members. Under the Laws Divine and Martial, or under Dale's Laws, military rule prevented the administration of justice according to the laws of England, as ordained by the charters of 1606 and 1609.[1]

---

[1] P. A. Bruce, *Institutional History of Virginia in the Seventeenth Century*, I, 647-52.

PROVOST-MARSHAL, FORERUNNER OF THE SHERIFF

During this period of government by military law the absence from the records of any mention of the sheriff or any civil official corresponding to the sheriff is not strange. The provost-marshal of this period, whose name was taken by the forerunner of the sheriff between 1619 and 1634, is mentioned in Dale's Laws and in the proclamation of February 20, 1617/18, appointing William Cradock provost-marshal of Burmuda City, but he is purely a military official.[2] In this capacity, as commander of the fortifications and forces of the colony, Sir William Newce appears in the period 1619-34.[3]

The introduction of self-government in 1619 was soon followed by what can accurately be called "a judicial system." The General Court now began to function as first intended, deciding the most important civil and criminal cases, while monthly courts, later called county courts, were created by the Assembly from time to time under the ordinance of 1618 for the various groups of settlements in the colony. The monthly courts were given jurisdiction over the less important civil and criminal cases in the outlying precincts and thus assisted the General Court in dispensing justice conveniently and cheaply in all parts of the colony.[4] They were presided over by the commander and three or more commissioners

[2] Peter Force, *Tracts,* III, No. 2; *Virginia Magazine of History and Biography,* IV, 29.

[3] *Collections of the Virginia Historical Society,* VII-VIII, 120.

[4] Bruce, *Inst. Hist. of Va.,* I, 484-86.

QUALIFICATIONS AND APPOINTMENT 65

who, after 1634 when the settlements were grouped by statute into counties, held the county court.

With the functioning of the General Court, or Quarter Court, as the highest court in the colony next to the General Assembly was now called for several decades, and with the establishment of monthly courts[5] the true ancestor of the sheriff appears, though he was known by the title of provost-marshal and marshal until the counties were formed in 1634. The provost-marshal is merely mentioned in the proceedings of the Assembly of 1619. In 1621 the Council in London, after receiving much complaint of the high fees exacted by provost-marshals and jailers, ordered their limitation by the Governor and Council.[6] The instructions contained in the commission to the head of the monthly court, the commander, together with the records of the proceedings of the early assemblies and quarter courts between 1619 and 1634, though meagre and insufficient to give us a complete account of the office, describe the provost-marshal as a civil officer, a court official, and the predecessor in early Virginia of the sheriff.

Duties of the Provost-Marshal

During these early years of the colony each group of settlements seems to have received in time its own monthly court and provost-marshal. The commission from Governor Yeardley in 1626 appointing

[5] By the Act of 1642/3 monthly courts were henceforth to be known as county courts, and the Quarter Court as the General Court by the Act of 1661/2.

[6] Virginia Miscellaneous Papers, 1606-80, p. 80.

Nathaniel Basse commander at Warrosquyoake ordered him to build a palisade for the protection of the inhabitants, to keep watch and ward at all times, and gave to him and several of the more influential settlers of his choice authority to hold a court with jurisdiction over misdemeanors and causes not exceeding one hundred pounds of tobacco in amount involved. The commander was to appoint a provost-marshal to assist him by keeping a register of all persons delinquent, of those who died, and of fines. The provost-marshal was also required to appraise and return an inventory of deceased persons to the Governor and Council within twenty days after their death, and, on warrant from the commander or from any two of the commission, to apprehend and convey to Jamestown all felons.[7]

From the records extant of the early General Court and the Assembly we learn that the provost-marshal received prescribed fees in pounds of tobacco for making an arrest, so much for warning to the court, and so much for imprisoning, for laying by the heels, whipping, pillorying, ducking, etc.[8] As a court official the provost-marshal also impanelled juries;[9] received fines of the court; presented drunkards to the court,[10] later a duty of the church-

[7] Edmund Randolph MS, 1626-34; Split by copyist on sheets 12 and 13. This was the early form of the commission of the peace in Virginia.
[8] *Va. Mag. of Hist. and Biog.*, IV, 23; XXVII, 34; W. W. Hening, *The Statutes-at-Large, being a Collection of all the Laws of Virginia, 1619-1792*, I, 176-77, 201, 220.
[9] *Va. Mag. of Hist. and Biog.*, XXI, 54.
[10] *Ibid.*, IV, 24.

QUALIFICATIONS AND APPOINTMENT 67

wardens; and was often appointed by the court to act on committees of appraisal and to return inventories of such to the courts.[11] Since most of these duties belonged at a later date to the sheriff, this fact, together with the certainty that for some time after the creation of the office the sheriff was referred to without distinction as provost-marshal and marshal, strongly indicates that this official had early done the sheriff's work.[12]

EARLY PROVOST-MARSHALS AND SHERIFFS

Of all the provost-marshals and early sheriffs only a few names survive. Randall Smallwood was provost-marshal for three successive years, 1625-27, and Richard North is mentioned as one of the early marshals of Accomac.[13] Though William Stone was sworn sheriff of Accomac by the terms of an order from the Governor and his Council dated March 14, 1633/4, requiring sheriffs to be appointed throughout the colony,[14] the records of Accomac of September, 1634, contain a command by the county court of payment of a fine of five shillings to Walter Scott, provost-marshal.[15] It is unlikely that Stone served as sheriff much of that year, for his name appears in most of the lists of commissioners, or justices of the peace,[16] present at the meetings of the

[11] *Ibid.*, XIII, 389-90; XXIII, 14; XXV, 235; XXVIII, 99.
[12] *Ibid.*, III (1638), 27; Accomac County Records, 1632-40, p. 44.
[13] Accomac County Records, 1632-40, p. 11.
[14] *Ibid.*, p. 18.   [15] *Ibid.*, p. 20.
[16] "Commissioners" were renamed "justices of the peace" by the Act of March, 1661/2.

county court of Accomac. Another of the early sheriffs was William English, the sheriff of York, reported to have been one of the chief speakers, Captain Martin and Francis Pott being the other two, who incited the crowd at York in April, 1635, against Governor Harvey.[17]

In 1634 Virginia was divided by statute into eight shires, to be governed like the English shires and to have sheriffs with the same power as in England.[18]

Property Qualifications

The choice of sheriffs was confined almost entirely to the larger landowners in the counties. This group, like the English country gentry, filled the important county offices and represented the county in the lower house of the Assembly but, unlike the English county families, monopolized, for the sake of their fees, the less important offices also. The same names appear in the county court records as justices of the peace, sheriffs, county clerks, coroners, and surveyors, and the men who filled these positions were also the ones elected to the House of Burgesses and appointed to the Council and to other important executive positions at Jamestown.

Most of the influential men in Virginia served in one or more of the county offices and at some time as justice of the peace and sheriff. Included in the list of influential men was Captain John Sibsey of Lower Norfolk County, who had been a member of

[17] Sainsbury Papers, 1631-37/8, pp. 101, 102, 126. Printed in *Va. Mag. of Hist. and Biog.*, I, 425-26; VIII, 303.
[18] Hening, I, 224.

the House of Burgesses before his appointment to the Council in 1636/7, and who in the years following served as commander of his county, as commissioner, as burgess, and as sheriff.[19] Captain William Stone of Accomac, who has already been mentioned, had an even more distinguished career. He was appointed sheriff in 1634, again in 1645, and during most of the interval served as one of the commissioners in his county.[20] In 1648 he moved to Maryland, was appointed governor by Lord Baltimore, and thereafter played an important part in the political life of that colony.

Among the more eminent public men of the later period were Colonel Thomas Swann, who was elected several times to the House of Burgesses, appointed sheriff of Surry in 1652, again in 1653, and a few years later to the Council;[21] Captain Daniel Parke of York, a member of the county bench for some time before becoming sheriff in 1659, who was later appointed to the Council and then became secretary of state in 1678, which office he held up to his death in the following year; Colonel Edward Hill, the younger, who was sheriff of Charles City County in 1661, before that a member of the Council, and afterwards attorney-general, treasurer, and speaker of the House of Burgesses; John Custis I, sheriff of Northampton in 1659 and a member of the Council in 1677; Colonel Isaac Allerton, justice of the peace in Northumberland in 1663, a member of the House

---

[19] *Va. Mag. of Hist. and Biog.*, VIII, 197.
[20] Accomac County Records, 1632-40; *ibid.*, 1640-45.
[21] *Va. Mag. of Hist. and Biog.*, III, 154.

of Burgesses in February, 1676/7, a member of the Council in 1683, and sheriff of Westmoreland in 1685 and 1686; Colonel Christopher Wormeley, who was sheriff of Middlesex in 1674 and 1681 and a member of the Council in 1683; and Colonel Edmund Scarborough, who was sheriff of Accomac in 1663 and surveyor-general from 1665 to 1671. An examination of the county court and other records[22] shows that these officials had served at some time during their lives as justices of the peace and as members of the House of Burgesses.

The alternation of the planters between the offices of justice of the peace and of sheriff is very conspicuous in the county court records. It is unusual to find a sheriff whose name does not appear both before and after his term of office in the lists of the justices of the peace. This close association was strengthened by the custom arising several years before 1660 of the planters' regularly taking their turns as sheriffs and afterwards returning to the bench. By the Act of 1660/1, which provided that commissioners be appointed to the office of sheriff in the order of their seniority in commission, this practice of rotation in office was legalized.[23] The official career in his county of Colonel Anthony Lawson was somewhat longer than that of most of his class but ran the course of most planters, especially after 1660,

[22] The lists of burgesses and appointments to the Council and to other executive positions at Jamestown have been copied from the lists compiled by William G. and Mary Newton Stanard in the *Colonial Virginia Register*.
[23] Hening, II, 21.

when the sheriff's office was often held for several consecutive years by the same person. Lawson was justice of the peace in Lower Norfolk County from February, 1672/3, to May, 1682, sheriff of Lower Norfolk from 1682 to 1685 inclusive, justice of the peace again in that county from May, 1687, to May, 1691, and in Norfolk County to May, 1693, sheriff of Norfolk County from May, 1693, to May, 1695, and a justice in Princess Anne County from November, 1696, to July, 1701.[24]

The chief qualification for appointment to the shrievalty in Virginia, then, as in the English counties was inclusion within the group of larger landowners. In both countries the basis of this restriction was primarily financial but was viewed from two different angles. As will be seen more clearly later, the planters were anxious to share the office among themselves for its good fees; the English government, on the other hand, felt obliged to confine its appointments largely to this class in the county, not from any regard for its material welfare, for the office was usually a financial burden, nor so much because its members were of the better class socially, but for the very good reason which we have already pointed out—they were best able to meet the expenses of the office.

OTHER RESTRICTIONS

The restrictions on the office were about the same as those prevailing in England at the time. By his

[24] *Lower Norfolk County Virginia Antiquary,* I, 47 n. Lower Norfolk County was divided into Norfolk and Princess Anne counties in 1691.

oath of office the sheriff was required, unless otherwise licensed by governor and Council, to reside in the county during his term. Because of this requirement he was forbidden by a number of statutes from being at the same time a burgess or councillor. On the other hand, new elections were constantly being necessitated by reason of the appointment of certain burgesses to the sheriff's office.[25] In March, 1659/60, the Assembly provided against its dismemberment through burgesses' being made councillors or sheriffs before its dissolution, by prescribing a fine of ten thousand pounds of tobacco for such contempt.[26]

The Act of 1660/1, as we have noticed, restricted the choice of sheriff to members of the county bench. To comply with this law a planter was sometimes first sworn justice of the peace and then sheriff at the same court, but he could not serve both offices at the same time. The sheriff was likewise forbidden, along with other county officials, from pleading as an attorney in any court to which he belonged while the party for whom he appeared resided in the colony.[27]

Method of Appointment

From the earliest date appointment was by the governor, acting with the advice and consent of the Council.[28] Nevertheless, the county commissioners

[25] *Journals of the House of Burgesses of Virginia, 1619-1658/9*, p. 97; Hening, I, 407, 414, 493.
[26] *Ibid.*, I, 540-41.
[27] *Ibid.*, I, 330, 523; II, 81.
[28] Randolph MSS, III, 225, 233; Accomac County Records, 1632-40, p. 18; Sainsbury Papers, 1631-37/8, p. 184.

QUALIFICATIONS AND APPOINTMENT 73

had much to say regarding the selection, and more as time went on, until the Act of 1660/1 was passed providing that the sheriff's place be conferred on the first in commission "and so devolve to every commissioner in course."[29]

While a statute of 1654 provided that the commissioners recommend three or more persons from whom the governor and Council were to choose one as sheriff,[30] this indirect method of appointment was practised from the beginning. At the Accomac County court held in September, 1636, six names were selected by the commissioners for presentation at the next Quarter Court to the governor and Council; at the November court of the following year, three names; and at the May court in 1639, three, but in May, 1641, the commissioners nominated ten persons, four of whom—Argoll Yeardley, Nathaniel Littleton, Obedience Robins, and William Stone—had been for some time leading members of the Accomac County bench. However, it soon became the custom for the commissioners to nominate only three, and these from their own number, usually at the last county court before the meeting of the General Court in the spring. At this time the governor "pricked" one from these for sheriff.[31]

Two interesting departures from this otherwise

[29] Hening, II, 21. The substance of this act is repeated in the statute of 1661/2.
[30] *Ibid.*, I, 392.
[31] Lower Norfolk County Records, 1646-51, pp. 142, 174[2]; Northampton County Records, 1654-55, p. 3[2]; York County Records, 1657-62, pp. 52, 77, etc.

quite regularly followed election system are noted in the county records. Acting on a proclamation of March 13, 1651/2, commanding each county to choose its sheriff, the commissioners of Northampton County asked the inhabitants of that county to elect. This they did, and the popular election being duly approved, Mr. William Waters became sheriff of the county.[32] The entry reads: "that this day Leift. Wm. Waters a gent. According to the Instruccons directed to ye Comissions & Inhabitants of this County By Pluralitye of voyces was nominated & made choyce of to bee high sherr of Northampton Countie from this p^{r}sent daye dureinge ye accustomed tyme."[33] This is an interesting return to the practice during the last years of Edward I and the early part of the reign of Edward II, when sheriffs were elected by the counties. It may have been a part of the plan of the Commonwealth to democratize county government, as evidenced by the increase in the number of justices at this time, but if so the idea must for some reason have been abandoned very soon, for we find no other accounts of this nature. The other exception is found in the records kept of the proceedings of the first court of Lancaster in January, 1652/3, and was due to the immediate need of a sheriff for the new county. The commissioners appointed John Philips clerk of the court, and then, in consideration of the fact that the county was in its infancy and hardly able to afford a livelihood to

[32] Northampton County Records, 1651-54, p. 66.
[33] *Ibid.*, p. 63^2.

QUALIFICATIONS AND APPOINTMENT 75

anyone who should officiate as sheriff, gave him that office also.[34]

ADMISSION TO OFFICE

The prominent part taken by the commissioners, or justices of the peace, in the process of appointment continued throughout the induction into office. After the "pricking" of the sheriff, the General Court commanded him to be sworn, usually at the next county court. Here, presumably in the court room, the sheriff produced his commission signed by the secretary before the justices and then took the oaths of office, and of Allegiance and Supremacy. In case the next court convened too late, the governor directed a *dedimus* to three or four justices of the peace for taking these oaths out of court.[35] After giving security to the justices for the performance of his duties, particularly of accounting for the revenues entrusted to his collection, the sheriff was admitted to office.[36]

[34] *William and Mary College Quarterly,* XX, 132-33; Morgan P. Robinson, *Virginia Counties: Those Resulting from Virginia Legislation,* p. 83.

[35] Charles City County Records, 1655-65, p. 102; Lower Norfolk County Records, 1646-51, p. 70; Accomac County Records, 1676-78, p. 171. In 1677 Jeffreys, for reasons not given, ordered the sheriff of Middlesex to summon a special court for the swearing of the new sheriff of that county.—Middlesex County Records, 1673-80, p. 88.

[36] The form of the bond given by the sheriff of Charles City County in 1661 is given in Charles City County Records, 1655-65, p. 268: "Coll Edward Hill esq^r & Capt Edward Hill confesse Judgemt in Co^{rt} to the Com^{rs} & Com of Charles Citty for 100000£^{s} of good tobb^o & caske to be pd to the sd Com^{rs} or any of them, or their successors ex^{e}tor adm^{rs}, als exec^o & costs. Conditionally that if the sd Com^{rs} & Com be secured and saved harmlesse & indempnified from all errors amisse

The whole process of nominating and appointing to office was clearly an adaptation of English methods. The few differences that appear can be attributed to the greater influence exerted on the proceedings by the colonial justices of the peace. The justices found in the good fees of the office, particularly in those for collecting the taxes, a strong incentive toward participation in the appointing of one from their number, which was usually lacking to the English justices of the peace. In general, county government in Virginia from the beginning functioned more independently of the central government than did county government in England.

IRREGULARITIES AND GRIEVANCES

Between 1660 and 1689, when the county courts and at least one governor, Berkeley, disregarded at times the laws governing appointment, the procedure was more irregular. When the counties were invited during the disturbance of 1676 to state their grievances to the Royal Commissioners their answers were much alike: that the sheriffs had continued in office longer than one year "so that they predominate over the poor comentrie,"[37] and their under-sheriffs often for three years or more; that offices of profit

or remisse pformance in the execucon of the office of sherr by the sd Capt. Edward the pent sherr of the sd Com & all colleccons legally comitted to his charge then ye sd Judgem^t to be void, & of none effect, or else to be in full force power & vertue. Test: Hool: Pryse cl   Edward Hill Junior Edw Hill"

[37] Isle of Wight grievances, Winder Papers, II, 183. Printed in *Va. Mag. of Hist. and Biog.*, II, 387-88.

QUALIFICATIONS AND APPOINTMENT 77

had been combined;[38] that clerks, justices of the peace, and sheriffs had been pleading in the courts they served; and that the sheriffs had been extortionate in their fees.

These complaints, some of which were incorporated into Bacon's *Laws*,[39] were well warranted according to the county court records. Before 1660 there were not many instances of sheriffs serving two years in succession, but after that date, though in violation of the statute of 1642/3, reënacted in 1657/8 and 1661/2, this practice became common, some of the planters serving as long as four years in succession. At the same time certain planters were especially favored by appointment to the shrievalty out of their turn, which also was illegal. In 1670 the justices of Northampton County petitioned and secured the continuance of Mr. William Mellinge in office on the ground that in his zeal for the thorough collecting of all the revenues entrusted him he had not found the opportunity to collect his own dues, which he would lose if not reappointed.[40] Some of the justices of York, in consideration of the great losses sustained by one of their number, Captain Ralph Langley, and that "ye sheriffs place may be a great help to him in this his p^{r}sent sufferinge condition" petitioned and secured from the governor his

[38] The County of Nansemond complained of the abuse of power possible to such persons as Lt. Col. Lear who had been at the same time clerk of the court, surveyor, escheat-master, and public notary, "being all places of pffitt & relyinge one on ye other."—Winder Papers, II, 206.
[39] Hening, II, 353-58.
[40] Northampton County Records, 1664-74, p. 86.

appointment in place of the one already appointed to the office.[41] Berkeley in 1677 was requested to appoint a sheriff for York out of the commission with the understanding that "it was Mr. John Page, his right to have had three years agoe, if the Justices had took it in Course."[42]

If for any reason a justice of the peace could not serve in his turn he frequently suggested someone to the governor in his stead, as did Colonel Cuthbert Potter of Middlesex in 1673 before his departure for England, in favor of Mr. Richard Robinson.[43] The justices of Northampton County in 1668 petitioned the governor to restore to the commission a colleague who had been left out because of his absence in England and to appoint him to the shrievalty for the ensuing year, the office being voluntarily resigned in his favor by Lieutenant Colonel Waters "who accordinge to precedency is the next." At the same time the justices recognized in their petition the right of the governor to choose whom he pleased, a privilege extended by the statute of 1661/2.[44] Berkeley certified his appointment in these words: "These are to certifie to you the Gent of Northton County that Mr. William Mellinge bee High Sheriffe of yor County for this ensuing yeare, and may also officiate in the place of Clerke accordinge to his Commission from the Secretary."[45]

[41] *William and Mary College Quarterly*, XIX, 198. A similar case is reported in the Stafford County Records, 1664-68, p. 75.
[42] York County Records, 1675-84, p. 9.
[43] Middlesex County Records, 1673-80, p. 10.
[44] Northampton County Records, 1664-74, p. 65.
[45] *Ibid.*

QUALIFICATIONS AND APPOINTMENT 79

While requests of this nature were usually granted, Berkeley, during his second term, from 1660 to 1677, showed some inclination to choose sheriffs and under-sheriffs without consulting the wishes of the justices of the peace. He appointed Captain John Robins sheriff of Northampton as a reward for his loyalty during the rebellion;[46] and he often disregarded the rights of the sheriff by appointing his under-sheriff.[47] There is enough evidence of this sort to indicate that the complaints from the inhabitants of Charles City County in 1677 to the Royal Commissioners to the effect that Berkeley had unlawfully taken upon himself the appointment to many offices of profit and had thus gained control over the more influential persons in the county, may well have represented the true state of affairs throughout the colony.[48]

The combining of offices of profit, another county grievance, was common after 1660. The sheriff was quite often the county clerk, as was Major Edward Dale, clerk of Lancaster from 1655 to 1674 and sheriff from 1668 to 1671 inclusive;[49] and William Mellinge and John Culpeper at the same time sheriff and clerk of Northampton in 1669 and 1672 respectively.[50] Before the creation of the coroner as a distinct official near the close of the period, the sheriff or the nearest justice performed his duties and re-

[46] *Ibid., 1674-79,* pp. 162-63.
[47] Surry County Records, 1645-72, p. 284; York County Records, 1664-72, pp. 131, 180, 341.
[48] Winder Papers, II, 326-27.
[49] Lancaster County Records, 1652-57, 1655-66, 1660-80.
[50] Northampton County Records, 1664-74, pp. 65, 125.

ceived his fees. Although the Assembly meeting in February, 1676/7, copied one of Bacon's *Laws* when it forbade the combining of offices, this harmful practice continued, as did also that of the sheriff and his deputy remaining in office for several successive years.[51]

THE UNDER-SHERIFF

After his induction into office the sheriff appointed his under-sheriff, from the class of small farmers apparently, who went through the same procedure in taking his oaths and giving bond to the justices of the peace.[52] By his contract with the sheriff the under-sheriff was bound to attend every county court and then, or soon after, to account to the high sheriff for his arrests, attachments, executions, and for everything else pertaining to the office; also to be present to receive the levies and to do his utmost in collecting them; and to cross the bay to attend the General Court at Jamestown if necessary to return writs or to do anything else appertaining to his office. In consideration of these services the under-sheriff was to have all his expenses paid and to receive as compensation one-half of the fees from the writs and bonds executed.[53] Captain William Stone agreed to pay his under-sheriff one-half of all his fees as sheriff, and of his allowances for collecting

[51] Accomac County Records, 1676-78, p. 171; 1678-82, p. 181. Lower Norfolk County Records, court of May, 1681. These records show the combining of the office of sheriff and surveyor.

[52] For his oath of office see *Va. Mag. of Hist. and Biog.*, XXIII, 227.

[53] Accomac County Records, 1640-45, p. 150.

QUALIFICATIONS AND APPOINTMENT 81

taxes, duties, levies, etc., but out of his half the under-sheriff, in turn, should pay one-third to his assistant.[54]

OTHER OFFICIALS

Before 1660 the sheriff, his under-sheriff, and deputy seem to have executed all the work of the office, but with the decided growth in population and the increasing business of the courts several other officials soon appeared, appointees of the sheriff. The sheriff also had his jailer, who frequently performed the duties of court crier as well. In 1679 the sheriff of Middlesex agreed to pay his jailer two thousand pounds of tobacco and cask for keeping the county prison and being answerable for all preventable escapes therefrom.[55] As regards the court crier, the sheriff and his under-sheriff seem to have performed this duty before 1660, but soon after that date the office of crier appears, sometimes as a separate office, but more often served by the jailer. In 1664 his salary in Northampton was fifteen hundred pounds of tobacco.[56] All three of these officials were appointed by the sheriff and paid for their services out of the county levies.

MARYLAND A PROPRIETARY COLONY

The foregoing discussion of the qualifications and appointment of the sheriff in Virginia applies with-

[54] Northampton County Records, 1645-51, pp. 20-21. See also the agreement between Edward Conaway, clerk and under-sheriff of Accomac in 1643 with his assistant.—Accomac County Records, 1640-45, pp. 239-40.
[55] Middlesex County Records, 1673-80, p. 176².
[56] Northampton County Records, 1657-64, p. 191.

out much variation to that official in Maryland. The source of his authority was different, and that difference should be borne in mind throughout this comparative study. Maryland was a proprietary not a royal colony, as was Virginia after 1624, and the sheriff's authority proceeded, therefore, from the Lord Proprietor and not from the King. The Baltimores were granted by their charter all the powers and privileges in the colony that had ever been exercised and enjoyed by the Bishop of Durham in the County Palatine of Durham. This was virtually a royal jurisdiction. A royal privilege incident to the grant and at that time enjoyed by the Bishop of Durham was the right of appointing the sheriff.

While the charter gave the Proprietor vast governmental powers, it also laid the foundations of popular government in the colony by providing that the Proprietor make the laws with the advice and assent of the freemen or their deputies whom he might call together as often as needed. The charter was granted to Cecilius Calvert, the second Lord Baltimore, in 1632; in March, 1633/4, the colonists landed at the mouth of the Potomac and began a settlement which they named St. Mary's. During the first few years the colony was ruled by the ordinances of the governor, Leonard Calvert, but the people were soon allowed to participate in their government—in a much shorter time, in fact, than in Virginia, where arbitrary government prevailed from 1607 to 1619.

The first regular assembly whose proceedings are

QUALIFICATIONS AND APPOINTMENT 83

known to us met at St. Mary's in January, 1637/8; those attending included the delegates from St. Mary's, St. George's, and Mattapanient hundreds, and from the Isle of Kent. These settlements at this early date made up the county of St. Mary's. By this time the Council was functioning in the threefold capacity of the Virginia Council, as an advisory body to the governor, as a part of the Assembly, later to be known as the Upper House, and, when sitting with the governor, who was chief justice, as the Provincial Court, the highest court in the province next to the Assembly. Only four years after the first settlement was begun, the executive, legislative, and judicial departments of the provincial government had emerged, though the development of later years had not been attained.

THE OFFICE OF COMMANDER

What system of local government was introduced? As previously stated, St. Mary's County at first included all the settlements, numbering the Isle of Kent, for all practical purposes, as one of its hundreds. Kent Island is not mentioned as a county until 1642.[57] At a very early date it was put under the civil and military control of a commander who, with the assistance of commissioners of the peace, constituted the government.[58] This concentration

[57] *Archives of Maryland: Proceedings and Acts of the General Assembly, 1637/8-1664*, pp. 183, 197. (Hereafter referred to as *Assembly Proceedings*.)

[58] The administration of Kent became the model for the two new counties formed in 1650, Ann Arundel and Charles, each with its commander and commissioners.—B. C. Steiner, *Maryland's First Courts*, p. 220.

of civil and military powers in the hands of one person seems to have been the form of government best suited to the needs of the sparsely populated and disturbed Kent as it had been best adapted to Virginia while in the process of developing her political and military systems. The commander of Kent, because of the great power with which he was endowed, has been likened to a deputy governor; however remarkable his authority, he is by no means to be considered as a new development in colonial government, for the Virginia commanders, before the establishment of the counties, were invested by their commissions with extensive civil and military powers.[59]

As local government in the two colonies developed, the importance of the commander as the military and civil head of the county declined. In Virginia his command over the militia was given by the middle of the century to other military officials, and in the county court he was reduced from the presidency of the court to become an ordinary justice of the peace awaiting his turn to preside. In Maryland the commanders, the best known of whom are the commanders of Kent, gradually disappeared soon after the Restoration.

Formation of Counties

Four counties had been formed by 1651, St. Mary's, Kent, Ann Arundel, and Charles, and apparently only three distinct county courts, for the

[59] Hening, I, 131, 140, 227; Edmund Randolph MS, 1626-34, sheets 12 and 13.

QUALIFICATIONS AND APPOINTMENT 85

county court of St. Mary's seems to have been united with the Provincial Court until 1659 or 1660.[60] Before the year 1689 ten counties had been organized along the eastern and western shores of Chesapeake Bay. To St. Mary's, Kent, Ann Arundel, and Charles had been added Calvert and Baltemore, and on the eastern shore four counties had been carved out of the original Kent County in the order given: Talbot, Dorchester, Somerset, and Cecil. In each county was a county court presided over by the commander and commissioners, or justices of the peace, later by the justices alone. As in Virginia the county court became the focal point of county government.

THE HUNDRED AS A GOVERNMENTAL UNIT

Of the first four counties formed, St. Mary's alone was divided into hundreds, the others probably being too sparsely settled for subdivision;[61] after 1660 the hundred was the next political subdivision in all the counties. In Virginia the hundreds, or groups of plantations with ill-defined boundaries, formed the governmental units before the establishment of counties in 1634; after that date their place as such was taken by the counties, the first eight of which were organized in that year. But the counties of Maryland were divided into hundreds according to the English scheme of government, and the hundreds given probably a greater usefulness than they pos-

---

[60] *Proceedings, Judicial and Testamentary Business of the Provincial Court, 1658-62*, pp. 342-43. (Hereafter referred to as *Provincial Court Proceedings*.)

[61] L. W. Wilhelm, *Local Institutions of Maryland*, p. 349.

sessed at this time in England. They served not only as fiscal districts and as military areas, but, in addition, before 1654 as units of representation. The few noteworthy divergences in the office of sheriff in Maryland are traceable first, to the use of the hundred as the election unit, which it had never been in England and which it ceased to be in Virginia after the establishment of county government; and secondly, to the extraordinary powers given to the early commanders.

County Government in Maryland

County government in Maryland was similar in most respects to county government in Virginia. Indeed, there appeared in Maryland so many of those divergences from English institutions and practices found in Virginia that we are tempted into saying that Maryland copied from the institutions of the older colony. The decided similarity in environment, however, was bound to influence the colonists toward the construction of closely approximating political systems.

The office of commissioner, or of justice of the peace, corresponded very closely to that of the Virginia justice of the peace. The coroner did not appear as a distinct official until 1666, his duties prior to that date being performed by the sheriff.[62] His chief work was the holding of inquests, though he was sometimes assigned certain court duties of the

[62] *Proceedings of the Council, 1636-67,* pp. 61, 85; *Provincial Court Proceedings, 1637-50,* p. 254; *1649/50-57,* p. 74; *1658-62,* p. 482.

QUALIFICATIONS AND APPOINTMENT 87

sheriff when the latter was derelict of duty or party to a suit in the county court.[63] The county clerk kept the county records, issued court papers, helped direct trial proceedings, and made himself otherwise useful to the justices of the peace. The other important county official besides the justice of the peace, the coroner, and the clerk, was the county court's chief executive officer, the sheriff.

THE SHERIFF IN MARYLAND

A sheriff was appointed to each county with the exception of Charles, which was for a short period under the sheriff of St. Mary's.[64] In the early years of the colony the sheriff was sometimes called "marshal."[65] His chief qualification for office was the same as in Virginia and England, that he be of sufficient estate. The choice was restricted to the group of planters in the county. The larger landowners were the political leaders in Maryland as they were in Virginia. They were appointed to the Council and Upper House, and elected as delegates to the Lower House. In the counties they monopolized the offices of justice of the peace, clerk, coroner, and sheriff, and at times served as high constables and deputy surveyors.[66] An examination of the county

[63] *Proceedings of the Council, 1681-85/6,* p. 326; *Provincial Court Proceedings,* Liber N. N., 1675-79, p. 845; Kent County Records, 1676-95, court order of March, 1697.

[64] *Provincial Court Proceedings, 1649/50-57,* p. 124; *1658-62,* pp. 86, 194.

[65] *Assembly Proceedings, 1637/8-64,* p. 163.

[66] Robert Vaughan, one of the most prominent of the early settlers, served for a time as high constable of St. George's Hundred.—*Assembly Proceedings, 1637/8-64,* p. 2.

court records alongside the provincial records shows the regularity with which the planters alternated between the offices of justice of the peace and sheriff. Their domination over these two offices seems to have been quite as complete in Maryland as in Virginia.[67]

The restrictions on the office were the same as in Virginia. The sheriff could not during his term of office sit in the Assembly;[68] he was forbidden to hold the office of clerk and of deputy surveyor while sheriff, or to act as an attorney in the courts he served.[69] Though he was prohibited from holding office longer than one year, the laws governing this[70] were often disregarded. Certain planters were favored with the office for three and four successive years. Emboldened by long continuance in office, they extorted from the people so shamefully that the Assembly in 1678 passed a law to the effect that thereafter no sheriff or under-sheriff should continue in office longer than one year unless he first presented to the Council a certificate from the county court attesting his honest and efficient execution of the office during the preceding year.[71] The numerous complaints against the sheriffs suggest that the

[67] *Proceedings of the Council, 1667-87/8*, p. 462; *1671-81*, p. 345; *1681-85/6*, p. 406; Kent County Records, 1657-62.

[68] *Assembly Proceedings, 1678-83*, pp. 63, 134, 451, 529, 531; *Proceedings of the Council, 1667-87/8*, p. 495.

[69] Laws of 1666. John Morgan was appointed sheriff and clerk of Talbot in 1662—*Proceedings of the Council, 1636-67,* p. 449; and Stephen Horsey was appointed sheriff and deputy surveyor of Somerset in 1666.—Somerset County Records, Liber B I, 1665-68, p. 24.

[70] Acts of 1661 and 1662.

[71] *Assembly Proceedings, 1678-83*, pp. 68-69.

QUALIFICATIONS AND APPOINTMENT 89

nominations by the justices were often dictated by selfish motives rather than by careful appraisals of the qualifications of the nominees.[72] For gross abuse of his office the Lower House in 1676 impeached Charles James, high sheriff of Cecil County, before the Upper House. He was convicted, sentenced to lose his commission, and to be thereafter disabled from holding any public office.[73]

THE CASE OF EDWARD SWEATNAM

The controversy over the appointment of Edward Sweatnam of Kent County is worth mentioning, not so much because of his long service of four years in office, which was not so unusual at that time, as for the differing opinions it gives of the political leaders of that day concerning the right basis for the choice of sheriff. The justices of Kent had certified to the Council that Sweatnam had behaved himself civilly in office and that there were no complaints against him.[74] Yet the Council was divided on the matter of his reappointment. The treasurer, Colonel Lowe, argued that someone else "should participate of his Lordship's favour," Sweatnam having had the "benefitt of that Place this 4 year." He proposed the appointment of Allan Smith as one having sufficient property. Colonel Darnall replied that Smith did not possess Sweatnam's qualifications of long residence and sufficient property, and he thought

[72] *Proceedings of the Council, 1671-81,* pp. 201-3; *Assembly Proceedings, 1666-76,* pp. 222-23, 244, 254; *1684-92,* p. 468.
[73] *Ibid., 1666-76,* pp. 480, 491, 496, 499.
[74] Kent County Records, 1676-95, p. 130².

it a bad policy to displace one "whoe had given good proofe of his diligence and honesty to adventure on an uncertainty." The Council finally decided by majority vote to discharge Sweatnam and appoint Smith in his place for the ensuing year.[75] Sweatnam complained to Lord Baltimore, who in reply sharply rebuked the members of the Council. It was poor judgment, he declared, to remove one who had behaved himself so well in office in favor of an inexperienced person. Such was not his policy for he "ever took care to continue good men in their places as an encouragement to such to continue Just and faithful."[76]

Lord Baltimore's ideas on office-holding were in strong contrast to those held by most lawyers in England, Virginia, and Maryland, who opposed continuance in the sheriff's office longer than one year as too great an encouragement to graft.

Appointment and Induction

Since the method of appointment in Maryland was the same as in Virginia, it need not be discussed in such detail. A law of 1642 provided that before the end of the March court the councillors, if sitting in the Provincial Court, or the commissioners, if in the county court, should recommend to the governor the names of those best fitted to be sheriff, from which list, or at his discretion, the governor should select one.[77] The Act of 1661 established the prac-

---

[75] *Proceedings of the Council, 1667-87/8,* pp. 543-44.
[76] *Ibid., 1687/8-93,* pp. 15-16.
[77] *Assembly Proceedings, 1637/8-64,* p. 148.

QUALIFICATIONS AND APPOINTMENT 91

tice of the justices' nominating at their March courts three persons, from whom the governor chose one.[78] The only exceptions were in Kent, Ann Arundel, and Charles counties, where for a time the commanders were given the privilege of appointing the sheriff.[79]

Immediately after the sheriff's appointment the secretary made out and sent down his papers: his patent of office with oath attached, a writ of assistance giving him the power of the county, a writ of discharge for his predecessor in office, his bond, and a warrant to take the list of tithables.[80] All these papers, with the exception of the one authorizing the sheriff to take the list of tithables, were the official papers of the sheriff in England and Virginia. The induction into office took place, as in Virginia, before the justices in the county court, or before several justices especially commissioned, out of court.

The sheriff's chief assistant was his under-sheriff. The under-sheriff was appointed by the sheriff from the smaller landowners and professional men and paid a certain per cent of the fees of the office for executing writs, warrants, summonses, etc.[81] In St.

[78] *Ibid.*, p. 412. See also *Proceedings of the Council, 1636-67*, pp. 448-49, 514, 517, 526-27, etc.
[79] Commission of Giles Brent, commander of Kent Island, *Proceedings of the Council, 1636-67*, pp. 88-89; of Robert Brooke of Charles County, *ibid., 1636-67*, pp. 237-40, 308; of Edward Lloyd, commander of Ann Arundel county, *ibid., 1636-67*, pp. 257-58.
[80] *Ibid., 1681-85/6*, p. 109; *1636-67*, pp. 526-27; Baltemore County Records, Liber D, 1682-86, p. 150. Copies of the sheriff's patent of office are printed in *Proceedings of the Council, 1636-67*, pp. 96-97, 117.
[81] *Provincial Court Proceedings*, Liber F. F., 1665-69, p. 52.

Mary's County he was very early known as the bailiff, and there was one to each hundred.[82]

LEADERSHIP OF THE SHERIFF IN MARYLAND

The sheriff in Maryland was the county's civil head and most representative citizen. The quality of his leadership is well illustrated in the two following accounts: the justices of Dorchester had complained to the Council against the appointment of Major Taylor from the rank of sheriff over their heads to the presidency of the county court. The Council replied that Taylor, prior to his term as sheriff, had been in commission before any of the other justices of the peace, and that his removal to the shrievalty "and consequently to have the Command and charge of the whole County" was intended not to degrade him "but oneley a suspension of his acting by the said Com^{on} as a Justice in Court."[83] From the other account we learn that the basis of the sheriff's authority to determine the number of delegates to be elected was that he "did represent the body Aggregative of the County."[84]

[82] *Proceedings of the Council, 1636-67*, p. 117.
[83] *Ibid., 1681-85/6*, p. 406. This account depicts perhaps better than any other the alternation of the planters between the offices of justice of the peace and sheriff, an outstanding characteristic of county government in both colonies.
[84] *Assembly Proceedings, 1637/8-64*, p. 398.

Chapter VII
COURT SERVICE
The Oath of Office

THE OATH of the colonial sheriff repeats many of the duties to which the English sheriff was sworn and in almost the same words. Like the English official, he was sworn to serve the King well and truly in his county; to keep the King's rights; to serve and return the King's writs honestly; to be just to the poor as well as the rich, and to disturb no man's rights; to be responsible for the bailiff in his service; and, as in England, to be resident within his county during his term of office, unless otherwise licensed by the governor and Council. The other duties of the sheriff are not specifically mentioned in his oath but are included in the final general obligation that he do all other things appertaining to his office to the utmost of his power.[1]

A Quarter Court, meeting at Jamestown in April, 1649, indicated other similarities when it declared the sheriffs to be "the kings deputyes within theire Countyes," charged to keep the King's peace and to suppress and punish malefactors in their counties; that the sheriff "may not bee abridged of any thing Incident or belonging to his office"; and that as regards the division of his work the "sherr may make his deputy for his under sherr, whoe in matters Con-

[1] Accomac County Records, 1640-45, pp. 72-73; Northampton County Records, 1664-74, p. 1.

cerning his Ministeriall office may wholly execute ye place in right of ye High-Sherr."[2]

The close similarity of their oaths and this declaration of the nature of the office, which reads so much like an excerpt from any of the English legal treatises of the time, when considered with the statute of 1634 declaring the power of the sheriff in Virginia to be that of the sheriff of any English shire, clearly indicate that the intention, at any rate, of the Virginians was to invest their official with all the legal rights and authority possessed by the English sheriff. However, further study reveals, besides conscious adoption as reflected in the many similarities in the two offices, the compelling force of certain differences in environment which prevented the colonial shrievalty from being an exact copy of the English office. On the other hand, these are not so numerous and marked as to make the two offices very unlike. The points of consonance with, and of departure from, the English shrievalty appear in a consideration of his duties in the following chapters as an executive official of the courts, as the chief medium of governmental communication, as collector of revenues, and as conservator of the peace.

Organization of Courts

The sheriff was, above all else, a court official. By far the greater part of his work he and his deputies performed as the executive officers of the General

[2] Lower Norfolk County Records, 1646-51, p. 112^2.

Court and the county courts.[3] In England the sheriff, on command of the justices of the peace, commanded, through his bailiff in each hundred, the attendance of the King's officials in the county and of the parties in the case, and notified all freeholders with annual income of a certain value to attend quarter-sessions and the assizes; in Virginia his notices were not required to be so widespread, for the obligation there to attend seems to have been borne by a much fewer number—the active participants in the court proceedings, who were notified individually. This seems true of the regular sessions of the county courts whose dates of meeting were set by law,[4] as also of the courts called in special session to decide matters of public concern, such as the best place for building a courthouse or the revision of a levy, or called at the request of certain merchants who for urgent business reasons needed a quick settlement of their suits. The Northampton County court, for example, met as often as eleven times during 1644, which was quite in excess of the legal requirement of six meetings a year.[5] For summoning to a private court the justices and witnesses, and securing the attendance of his officers, a county court of Westmoreland in 1687 ordered the sheriff paid one thousand pounds of tobacco with costs of suit,[6] a fee customarily paid in Lower Norfolk County until reduced

[3] The Sheriff of James City County was Sergeant-at-Arms to the General Assembly.—Hening, I, 503.
[4] Acts of 1642/3, 1657/8, and 1661/2.
[5] Bruce, *Inst. Hist. of Va.*, I, 520.
[6] Westmoreland County Records, 1675/6—1688/9, p. 575.

by a court in 1685 to five hundred pounds plus the ordinary fees of summoning.[7]

The county court also met in special session as an orphans' court. Provision was made for this meeting of the justices by an act of the Assembly of March, 1642/3, which required all overseers and guardians of orphans to report at least once a year to the county court on the present condition of property in their charge.[8] The date of meeting was at the discretion of the justices, who usually convened the orphans' court shortly before or very soon after the regular meeting of the county court. A Lower Norfolk court, meeting on October 3, 1651, ordered that an "Orphans Court be kept the day after ye Endinge of the sd County Co^{rt}." and the "Shreive" to notify all whom it concerned.[9] On another occasion the sheriff was directed to give notice of both courts, the orphans' court preceding the other, when the commissioners, or justices, ordered all the guardians of orphans' estates to be summoned before them to give in their accounts on the 20th day of October next, that a court be held on the 26th for the trial of all other differences, and that all of the commissioners be notified by the sheriff to be present at these courts.[10] Nor was it safe for the guardians to disregard these summonses, for when the commission-

[7] Lower Norfolk County Records, 1675-86, court of Aug. 27, 1685.
[8] Hening, I, 261.
[9] Lower Norfolk County Records, 1646-51, p. 186.
[10] York County Records, 1638-48, p. 172, order of Sept. 26, 1646.

ers found by the sheriff's return that nine had failed to appear, they fined each of them two hundred pounds of tobacco for contempt.[11]

IMPANELLING OF JURIES

The sheriff was responsible for the organization of the courts, likewise for the smooth running of the machinery of justice. He summoned witnesses to court; defendants to appear to answer the charges against them; surveyors to bring in their presentments of persons delinquent in clearing their highways; burgesses of the county to attend for the making of by-laws; and all guardians and administrators to bring in their accounts.

In the process of court organization the sheriff impanelled all grand and petit juries. A statute of 1645 provided that a grand jury be impanelled at the March and midsummer county courts to attend and to receive all presentments and informations, to inquire of the breach of all penal laws and misdemeanors not affecting life or limb, and in case they found a true bill to bring the case before the county court for determination, or, if the reason were sufficient, before the governor and Council.[12] Besides the grand jury, the sheriff impanelled all other juries of inquiry: the coroner's jury, the escheator's jury, the jury of matrons, juries for the survey of boundaries in dispute, to determine the amount of damages inflicted on a certain piece of property, and to ap-

[11] *Ibid.*, pp. 184-85.
[12] Hening, I, 304. By Act of March, 1661/2, the dates were fixed for April and December.—*Ibid.*, II, 74.

praise the value of property in execution. In the colony, as in the mother country, both plaintiff and defendant had the right of jury trial, and it was the sheriff's duty to have twelve men ready for jury service during each day of court.[13] The jurors summoned by the sheriff were always to be "of ye Antientist and discreetest ffreeholders of ye Neighborhood."[14]

CHIEF EXECUTIVE OFFICIAL

The execution of the orders, judgments, and sentences of the courts comprised most of the work of the sheriff and his deputies. Scattered among the numerous court orders to arrest, to keep in safe custody, to whip, to summon to court, to attach, to serve execution on, to appraise, to put into possession, to pay the court award for not taking bail,[15] to collect officers' fees, and to outcry estates, are to be found in the county court records such varied duties as these: that the sheriff warn so-and-so not to sell any kind of drink;[16] that he take into his possession the estate of a drowned man until further order;[17] that he build prisons, stocks, and pillories; that he press

[13] *Ibid.,* Act of Nov., 1645; also Act of 1660/1.

[14] Middlesex County Records, 1680-94, pp. 265-66; *Minutes of the Council and General Court of Colonial Virginia,* p. 299.

[15] The entry most frequently met with in the county court records concerning the sheriff is the court order to him to produce the defendant at the next court or pay himself the court's award. This was required by many statutes which gave the sheriff the benefit of an attachment against the property of the defendant.—Hening, I, 271, 272, 305, 448; II, 62, 79, 169, 247-48.

[16] Lower Norfolk County Records, 1651-56, p. 186.

[17] Northampton County Records, 1657-64, p. 372.

boats and hands for the conveyance of prisoners and witnesses to Jamestown; that he receive the fines of those killing too few, and reward those who had killed more than the required number of crows;[18] that he take a stray beast into his custody until the rightful owner appear;[19] and that he notify the county of a runaway negro in his possession.[20] A schedule of fees was provided by statute to be paid the sheriff for the service of writs and other executive work.

As Administrative Official

In the performance of most of the duties mentioned above, the sheriff was no more than a servant of the courts—his work was entirely ministerial; but in the execution of other duties he was invested by the courts with some of the discretionary powers of an administrative official, though just how important or extensive these were one finds it difficult, as in judging the English sheriff, to determine. However, the following account may give some notion of his administrative work.

[18] Charles City County Records, 1655-65, p. 509.
[19] Northampton County Records, 1657-64, p. 52.
[20] "Northampton County: Whereas by his Excellencies Comaund I have in my Custody a Negro man of a Tall stature about 24 years of age or thereabouts and forasmuch as the Law Comaunds that Notice shall bee given of all such strayes in all publiq^e places within my Bayleywick. These are therefore to Informe all psons thereof, That if any man can lay just claime to the said Negro man he or they may have him payinge all just fees.
Dated this 2d of August 1688.
Then the above written sett up at court.
                    Jno Custis sheriffe Northt^{on} County"
—Northampton County Records, 1683-89, p. 387.

It was the sheriff's duty, on attachment, to seize as much of the property as would secure the debt and, in case of failure of replevy, to serve execution on the same. The procedure to be followed in determining what part of the property should be appraised, as also in selecting its appraisers, was somewhat irregular. A statute of February, 1644/5, gave to the commissioners the right to determine what part should be valued for satisfaction of the debt,[21] but a later Act of 1657/8, while prohibiting the debtor from giving up any part of the estate he pleased, provided that the sheriff seize any part, proceeding indifferently to both parties according to his oath. In case the sheriff and debtor differed, two or more of the commissioners were to decide.[22]

Appraisement was made either by two or more persons especially appointed, or by a jury of twelve men impanelled and sworn for that purpose. In the early days of the colony the provost-marshal was often appointed by the General Court to be one of a committee of appraisers; in 1632 this official was to be associated with one chosen by the executor or administrator, and the ten per cent fee for their services to be divided between them.[23] Nearly two years later, and shortly before the establishing of county government, Governor Harvey ordered Obedience Robins, commander of Accomac, to appraise the possessions of Henry Bagwell by a jury "of honest men

[21] Hening, I, 294.
[22] *Ibid.*, pp. 453-54.
[23] *Va. Mag. of Hist. and Biog.*, XIII, 389-90.

upon their oaths," and to make a return at the next Quarter Court.[24] But juries of appraisal seem not to have lasted long, for an Act of 1641 provided that the plaintiff and defendant should each choose two indifferent men and if they disagreed, then four or three of them should choose an umpire. This Act did not set a convenient time for the choosing of appraisers; so it was enacted in 1642/3 and reënacted in 1657/8 and in 1661/2 that in case either plaintiff or defendant neglected to appoint appraisers within three days' notice given them by the sheriff, it should be lawful for the sheriff to appoint for the one neglecting.[25] The duties of the sheriff in this procedure were completed after returning his writ and inventory to the court and putting the creditor in possession of the property found due him. The administrative duties of the sheriff were further increased by the court's appointing him, as though one of its members, to act as an administrator of estates.[26] When a sheriff reported that unless something were done part of the estate of the deceased would perish, the Northampton County court ordered him to act "as the Exigency of the present Condition of the said estate may require for the good & benefit thereof & give an acc^t. to the next Court."[27]

[24] Accomac County Records, 1632-40, pp. 16-17. The return ran: "According to this Warrant these goods were seised upon and praysed by these men heere expressed and delivered unto Petter Stafferton. [Names of the twelve follow]. Obedyence Robins Comdr."
[25] Hening, I, 259, 442; II, 80.
[26] Northampton County Records, 1664-74, p. 233.
[27] Ibid., 1674-79, p. 201.

Court Duties in Maryland

In Maryland the sheriff's court duties corresponded so closely that only a few, those which shed additional light on this subject, need be discussed.

The execution and return of writs and warrants comprised the bulk of his work in Maryland as in Virginia and England. The sheriffs in both colonies sought to avoid the hardships of travel to many homes and to those remotely situated in the county by waiting at the church doors to serve their warrants. But this seemed a desecration; besides, their presence frightened so many of those in danger of arrest away from the services that the colonial assemblies finally prohibited the practice altogether. The Maryland Assembly, for the same reason, also forbade the presence of the sheriff at the general musters.[28]

The return of a writ stating the action taken had to be made to the court from which the writ issued by the date specified.[29] For failure to return their writs according to court order the Provincial Court in 1678 fined each of the sheriffs of Dorchester, Charles, Calvert, Baltimore, Kent, and Ann Arundel counties two thousand pounds of tobacco.[30] Usually

[28] Hening, I, 457, Act of 1657/8; *Assembly Proceedings, 1637/8-1664,* p. 485; *1684-92,* p. 476, Acts of 1663 and 1692.

[29] A sheriff of St. Mary's returned to a writ of replevin, "The box of Cloathes two flitches of Bacon and the pott of butter within written I did replevin and did deliver the same to the within named Abell Jones. John Jarbo sher
The Rest of the goods were not to be found. John Jarbo sher."—*Provincial Court Proceedings,* Liber J. J. 1669-72, p. 2.

[30] *Provincial Court Proceedings,* Liber N. N., 1675-79, p. 655.

COURT SERVICE 103

the returns were written in English though a few were in Latin, like the return of a sheriff of St. Mary's to a writ of attachment: *nihil habet in Baliva mea*,[31] and the not infrequent return in actions of debt, *non est inventus*. Except during a few years of the Cromwellian period most of the English court records were written in Latin, but those of Virginia and Maryland, almost entirely in English. In addition to a few returns of writs the titles following the names of county officials were often written in abbreviated Latin as *cler. com.* for "county clerk," and *vic., subvic., subvice.*, and *subvice comes* for "sheriff" and "under-sheriff." One county clerk capitalized on his classical learning by writing spryly on the flyleaf of a volume of court judgments, *"Johes Thompson cler com cecil."*[32]

The colonial county courts made the sheriff responsible for the building and repair of the stocks, pillory, whipping post, and ducking stool. The justices of Charles County in 1663 ordered the sheriff to set up the ducking stool at Mr. Pope's Creek and the stocks, pillory, and whipping post at the courthouse, where they were usually kept.[33] The sheriff, or someone appointed by him, inflicted the punishments prescribed by the county court. The court records contain numerous orders to the sheriff like the following: to put Thomas Norcombe in the pillory for his second offense of hog-stealing "the full

[31] *Provincial Court Proceedings,* Liber B. B., 1663-65, p. 398.
[32] Cecil County Records, 1692-96.
[33] Charles County Records, 1662-65, p. 112.

time & space of 4 hours";[34] to give a certain Hamball and Elisabeth Spicer five lashes apiece for slandering John Courts;[35] and to nail John Goneere by both ears to the pillory, with three nails in each ear, and afterwards to whip him with twenty "good lashes" for perjuring himself.[36]

DIGNITY OF COURT OFFICIALS

Disrespect to the court was always punished. It is doubtful if the judges in England defended the dignity of their office with any greater watchfulness and austerity than did the members of the colonial county bench. The justices of Kent, meeting on the first day of September, 1658, directed the sheriff to publish this order, that "whereas It is the Costome of England, grounded upon the word of God that due respect be given to Maiestrates—that noe man p^{r}sume, excepte a member of the Court, to stand wth his hat on his head, in the p^{r}sence of the Court, whilst the Court is sitting or use any onscivell Language, upon paine of such ffine & other punishm^t as the Court shall thinke fit."[37] When the justices at the November sessions spied Henry Carline standing in court with his hat on, they fined him three hundred pounds of tobacco, even though he was a prominent planter who had a few years before this incident served as justice of the peace and as sheriff of Kent

---

[34] Dorchester County Records, 1689-92, order of Feb. 5, 1691/92.
[35] Charles County Records, 1658-62, p. 26.
[36] *Provincial Court Proceedings, 1637-50*, p. 393.
[37] Kent County Records, Liber B, 1658-62, p. 119.

County.[38] A Baltemore court ordered the sheriff to put in the stocks one who had used "mean words" to the court,[39] and the Dorchester justices had the sheriff of that county give Matthew Carey ten lashes "well laid on his bare back," who also had to pay a fine of five hundred pounds of tobacco, for uttering false reports against John Brooke, one of the justices of the court.[40]

The colonial justices were equally determined that the sheriff receive due respect. Those of Kent ordered a warrant to be sent to the appropriate constable for bringing a certain James Lacey, servant, to answer to the justices for his abuse of Mr. Edward Sweatnam, the high sheriff,[41] and the justices of Lower Norfolk fined one who had abused the sheriff while in execution of his office four hundred pounds of tobacco.[42] "For opprobrious language uttered agst the sherr in contempt of his office & consequently of the authority whence it derives" the Charles City County court ordered that Benjamin Cartwright receive from the sheriff two lashes on his bare shoulders.[43] Here, of course, is the theoretical basis for the punishment of those found guilty of disrespect to the justices of the peace and the sheriff

[38] *Ibid.,* p. 131.
[39] Baltemore County Records, Liber F, 1691-93, p. 345.
For an interesting account of the manner in which the Virginia justices of the peace maintained the dignity of their court see Bruce's *Inst. Hist. of Va.,* I, 508-15.
[40] Dorchester County Records, 1689-92, order of Aug. 7, 1690.
[41] Kent County Records, 1676-95, p. 66. January, 1685/86.
[42] Lower Norfolk County Records, order of May 22, 1679.
[43] Charles City County Records, 1655-65, p. 140.

—that they served either under royal or proprietary commission and any indignity offered them was an offense to the King, or to the Proprietor, as the case might be.

The sheriff and justices of the peace carried the dignity of their offices into other public places than the county court. A seat had been reserved in the parish church of St. Mary White Chapel in Lancaster County for the justices and the sheriff. On one particular Sunday, while two justices and sheriff Edward Dale were occupying the seat, a certain Richard Price, whose motive is not recorded, tried to intrude and thereby got into a scuffle with the sheriff "to the dishonour of God Almighty & contempt of his Majestie." It was no small offense, for the justices delivered Price over to the General Court to answer for his actions.[44]

The county clerks kept the court records decidedly too official to give us the personal characteristics of any of the sheriffs or justices of the peace. The official records, however, are about the only source of information we have, for the many diaries, journals, biographies, and letters which, with a bit of color here and there, portray the individuality of certain English county officials are unfortunately almost entirely lacking in the colonies.

Comparison with England

From the foregoing remarks on the colonial county court it is clear that this institution differed widely

[44] Lancaster County Records, 1666-80, order of November 8, 1671.

from any court in England. It possessed few of the characteristics of the English county court presided over by the sheriff. In organization the colonial county court was almost wholly different; in respect to relative importance, it was the focal point of county government while the sheriff's county court in England was, in the seventeenth century, a declining institution not to be compared in power and usefulness to the court of quarter-sessions. The colonial county court resembled most the English court of quarter-sessions. And yet while the general character of their administrative work was alike, the former possessed a much broader jurisdiction. The colonial county court decided under the common law civil suits up to a certain amount and the smaller criminal cases, while the English quarter-sessions tried criminal cases only. But the judicial authority of the Virginia justices extended far beyond the common law: it was equitable, maritime, and ecclesiastical. According to contemporary writers the justices tried causes belonging in England to the courts of Chancery, King's Bench, Common Pleas, Exchequer, Admiralty, and the ecclesiastical courts.[45] The justices of the peace in Maryland tried common law cases, sat as a court of chancery,[46] and probably had the other jurisdictions of the Virginia justices.

The greatest similarity between these two courts

[45] Hartwell, Chilton, and Blair, *An Account of the Present State and Government of Virginia, 1697-98*, section VII. (Hereafter referred to as *Present State of Virginia.*)

[46] *Md. Hist. Mag.*, VIII, 13; For ecclesiastical causes see *Proceedings of the Council, 1636-67*, p. 384.

most useful in the government of the county is to be found in the qualifications and the manner of appointment of the justices themselves. English quarter-sessions were presided over by justices of the peace appointed by the King from the country gentry; the colonial county court was held by commissioners, later called justices of the peace, who were appointed by the governor from the more influential planters in each county. In the care of these officials and of the sheriff, also appointed from this class, rested most of the work of county government in England and her two colonies.

Reasons for Legal and Institutional Divergencies

The more prosperous of the settlers in Virginia and Maryland found it possible to establish in the new world a landed aristocracy with social and political influence equal to and probably greater than that enjoyed by the English gentry in their counties, because the physical environment was favorable to the formation of large estates and to such a distinct social and political aristocracy. But it was their instinct to adopt as much of the social and political arrangements, of the laws, institutions, and practices of the mother country as the physical characteristics and the economic life of the colonies would allow. The cause assigned by William Fitzhugh for differences in the laws of Virginia was that "what Laws we have made amongst us here since our first Settlement are merely made for our particular constitution, where the Laws of England were thought inconvenient in that particular, and rather disadvantageous and burdensom than any way for our advantage or benefit."[47] This was also the reason for the differences that arose in colonial offices, in the judicial systems, the organization of each court, and in its procedure. There is much evidence in the records of the molding influence of physical and economic conditions.

In regard to jury trial the chief divergencies from English practice are to be found in the trial of the more serious criminal cases. In imitation of the English, who had given their counties the trial of capital offenses, an attempt was made to afford the inhabitants of Virginia counties equal court facilities, but the Assembly found this to be unjust and passed a law providing that such cases be tried at Jamestown and not in the counties, for these reasons: first, the population of any county in the colony was much smaller than that of any English county and consequently there were fewer qualified persons to choose from; and secondly, the jurors in the colony were much less practised in criminal cases, and besides had very little with which to inform themselves in case they erred. The statute of 1642/3 was therefore reënacted and the practice reëstablished that the sheriff keep all criminals in his custody until the first day of the Quarter Court or Assembly and then deliver them to

[47] Letter to Ralph Wormeley, June 9, 1683, *Va. Mag. of Hist. and Biog.*, I, 260. There was a marked tendency in both colonies to depart from the severe criminal laws of England.

the sheriff at Jamestown.⁴⁸ The same arrangement obtained in Maryland, of sending felons to St. Mary's for trial, and probably for the same reasons.

Though the laws of England required a jury of the vicinage for the trial of capital offenses, trial jurors in Virginia were drawn not entirely from the neighborhood but from two different sources. This was due to the fact that the courts at Jamestown were the only courts in the colony authorized to try felons, and the English law, if adopted, requiring jurors to have come long distances, would have entailed considerable hardship in travel and much expense to many persons. Instead of twelve persons, then, six were drawn from the neighborhood and six from those attending court.⁴⁹

COURT PROCEDURE MODELED AFTER ENGLAND

The colonies tried to adapt their court procedure as nearly to the English procedure as the environment would permit.⁵⁰ It was enacted in 1666 "for the

⁴⁸ Acts of 1655/6 and 1657/8.
⁴⁹ Act of 1661/2; *Va. Mag. of Hist. and Biog.*, I, 260. Letter of William Fitzhugh to Ralph Wormeley, 1683. See also Northumberland County Records, 1678-98, pp. 338-39.
⁵⁰ The opening of the circuit courts, which were held in 1662, is strongly reminiscent of the assizes: "Sylence being first Comanded on payne of Imprisonment the Commission granted by the Ho^ble his Maties Govern^r to Coll Edward Hill and Coll Thomas Swann to sitt as Itinerary Judges was Read & also the proclamacon under the said Itinerary Judges hands giving liberty to any person or persons having iust Complaint against any Justice of Yorke Comission or the whole Court for partiallity or Iniustice or against any officer of the Court Sherriffe or Clerke for non p formance of their office or Extortion of Fees since the last circuit of the Itinerary Judges to prosecute their Com-

better conformity of the proceedings of the courts of this country to the lawes of England" that the commissioners of the county courts send to England for the *Statutes at Large,* Dalton's *Justice of the Peace,* his *Office of Sheriff,* and Swinburne's *Book of Wills and Testaments.*[51] The court of Westmoreland, conforming to this law, and in response to its own special needs, ordered its clerk to send for these books as also for "Cooke upon Littleton" and for any others of use to the county which "will be of much use to informe our Judgmts in matters concerning judicature."[52] Laws were passed in Maryland ordering the county courts to send for Keeble's *Collection of the Statutes* and for Dalton's *Justice of the Peace.*[53] With these legal guides ever available the commission of the peace for Surry could justly require the justices to do "as near as may be according to the Laws and Customes of England and according to the Laws and Customes of this Country."[54] In 1686 the Henrico court ordered the commission of the peace to be published immediately after the opening of every court "to ye intent that ye Proceedings of our Courts may come as near as reasonably our

plaint & they should be heard, whose sylence at this Court to be a barr against all future claims or pretences and that being made hereafter shall make the Complainant lyable to an Action of Scandall."—York County Records, 1657-62, p. 168.

[51] Hening, II, 246.
[52] Westmoreland County Records, 1675/6-1688/9, p. 540.
[53] *Assembly Proceedings, 1678-83,* p. 70; *1684-92,* p. 521. Laws of 1678 and 1692.
[54] Surry County Records, 1684-6, p. 2.

psent condicon will admitt to ye practice of ye Courts in England."⁵⁵

The inhabitants of Maryland manifested a like disposition to be guided in their legislation and court procedure, whenever possible, by English laws and practices.⁵⁶

Advantages of Freer Environment

The salutary effect on court pleadings of a freer environment is indicated in a letter from Thomas Ludwell to Arlington in 1666, in which he described the General Court of Virginia as a court "wherein as greate care is taken to make the Lawes, and pleadings upon them easy & obvious to every mans und^r-standing as in other parts they doe to keep them a mistery to the people for noe advantage is allowed to either party from little errors in Declarations or pleas etc but both are kept within the just Lymmitts of ye merritts of their cause and judgm^ts pass secundum alegata et probata."⁵⁷

Both colonies adhered to the fundamentals of the procedure followed in the English courts but did away largely with those parts giving opportunity for trickery and vexatious delays.

Justice in the colonial courts was quicker and less

⁵⁵ Henrico County Records, 1677-92, p. 375. See also York County Records, 1684-87, p. 229; Council order, Colonial Office, Class 5, vol. 1405, p. 247. Printed in *Va. Mag. of Hist. and Biog.*, XII, 295-96.
⁵⁶ *Assembly Proceedings, 1637/8-64*, pp. 9, 31, 158, 448, etc. The Commission of the peace.
⁵⁷ Thomas Ludwell in his "Description of the Government of Virginia," 1666.—Winder Papers, I, 201-9.

expensive than in the courts in England. The author of *Leah and Rachel,* writing in 1656, was confident that in no place in the world could there be speedier and less expensive justice than in Virginia.[58] The first settlers in the colonies possessed considerable knowledge of English county government, but while they apparently tried to transplant to the colony the sheriff and other county officials with as slight a change in office as possible, they were forced to leave behind them in England forever a multitude of courts inherited from the Middle Ages, with their overlapping jurisdictions and confusing complexities of procedure.

Pioneer life demanded and produced a much simpler judicial system rising from the county court to the general court, or provincial court, and General Assembly, as also a more simplified procedure in these courts. Neither the sheriff's county court nor the hundred court found a place in such a system. These courts had outlived most of their usefulness in England and yet were retained alongside of quarter-sessions and the assizes, the courts which had stripped them of their early great authority. As for the manorial courts, though several were established in Maryland and lasted in that colony for some years, they seem never to have been introduced in Virginia. The reform of the judiciary came late in England; in Virginia and Maryland the English judicial system was reformed from the date of the establishment of civil government.

[58] Force, *Tracts,* III, No. 14.

Chapter VIII

AS A CHANNEL OF GOVERNMENTAL COMMUNICATION

PUBLICATION OF PROCLAMATIONS

THE SHERIFF was the chief means of governmental communication in Virginia and Maryland. We have observed that while the dates for the regular sessions of the county courts were settled by law, a county-wide notification not being required as in England, it was the duty of the sheriff to notify individually the justices of the peace, the guardians, and all others concerned to appear at special sessions of the county court. As organizer of the courts he impanelled all juries and summoned witnesses and the parties to the suit; he gave general notice of outcries, of surveys, to neglectful constables that they appear before the justices to take their oaths; and, in general terms, as the principal medium of communication within the county, he notified those concerned of the disposition of the courts he served.[1]

The sheriff was the chief connecting link between Jamestown and the counties. Although the statutes passed by the General Assembly did not provide for proclamation by the sheriff at markets, county courts,

[1] Richard Conquest, sheriff of Lower Norfolk County in 1648, in addition to performing his many court duties served as the executive officer of the vestry in that county. On one occasion he was ordered to notify the recent appointees and all other members of the vestry to be present at a meeting, and to summon "John Norwood to bee and appeare before the said vestry to give an Accompt of the proffitts of the Gleab land."— Lower Norfolk County Records, 1646-51, p. 82.

or at other public places, as was the case in England,[2] the publication throughout his county of orders and proclamations from Jamestown was a very important part of the sheriff's duties and probably the only part glorified with any of the high dignity and impressive ceremony displayed by the English sheriff when publishing royal proclamations or entertaining at the assizes.

There were proclamations by the governor against the destroying of tobacco plants, against riotous meetings, of the prorogation of the Assembly, and of writs of election *et cetera,* which were published by the sheriffs in county courts and in other public places, and in churches by the ministers. But only at the proclamation of a new king was there displayed any semblance of the county leadership and social preëminence characteristic of the English sheriff on ceremonial occasions. The accounts of the proclaiming of William and Mary at Jamestown may be well compared with that of James II in Kent, as described by Evelyn. Called to Bromeley by the sheriff to assist in the proclaiming of the King, Evelyn saw there the sheriff, the commander and several officers with five hundred troops, two trumpeters, and innumerable people. They marched into the market place with swords drawn, and there a ring being made, after sound of trumpets and silence

[2] The county courts and the people learned of the laws passed at the last Assembly from copies made of them and brought back from Jamestown by the clerks sent by the county courts for that purpose. Certain of these copies were at Hening's disposal in the compilation of his *Statutes-at-Large.*

made, the High Sheriff read the proclaiming titles to his bailiff, who repeated them aloud; then after the many shouts of the people "His Ma$^{ty's}$ health beeing drunk in a flint glasse of a yard long, by the Sheriff, Commander, Officers, and cheife Gentlemen, they all dispers'd."[3]

So detailed an account of the proceedings in the proclaiming of William and Mary in Virginia is unfortunately lacking, but enough has come down to us to indicate that the ceremony was quite as impressive, and enlivened with quite as much of the holiday spirit. The governor and Council at this time ordered "that tomorrow their most sacred Majesties, by Eleven of the Clock in the Morning, before the Court house Doore in James Citty, be Proclaimed King and Queene of England, France and Ireland & of the Territories and Dominions thereunto appertaining . . . and that the Sheriffe Sumons the best appearance that can be had at that time, for the Testifyeing the due Honour & Obedience, and acclamations of Joy, by fireing Great Guns, Sounding of Trumpets and beating of Drums."[4] The proclamation was to be made in like manner by the sheriffs in every county court in Virginia. The cost to the county of proclaiming Charles II in York was

[3] Evelyn, *Diary*, February 10, 1684/5. Interesting details of the banquet in Macclesfield, Cheshire, at the coronation of Charles II are to be found in the *Cheshire Notes and Queries*, New Series (1888), p. 185.

[4] Colonial Office, Class 5, vol. 1405, pp. 222-23. Printed in *Executive Journals of the Council of Colonial Virginia*, I, 106-7.

7,300 pounds of tobacco, including the expense of a barrel of powder, trumpeters, cannons, and nearly half of the whole expense, or 3,604 lbs., for 211 gallons of cider.[5]

ELECTION RESPONSIBILITIES

As in England the sheriff had entire charge of elections, his election duties in Virginia differing so little because the election system was so similar. Before 1634 the units of representation consisted of boroughs and hundreds, or plantations, but with the introduction of the county system of government in that year the county became the principal election district and continued as such throughout the period, the only other units of election being Jamestown, with its separate representation, and a few parishes in those counties notable for their gains in population.[6]

The whole election procedure followed the English model. When a new House was to be elected a summons in the name of the governor was sent out of the secretary's office to the sheriff in each county.[7] An Act of March 31, 1655, prescribed the course to be followed on receipt of the writ of election: within ten days afterward the sheriffs were to cause these to be published, and they or their deputies were to give notice to the voters from house to house of the day and week for choosing burgesses to serve in the

[5] York County Records, 1657-62, p. 96.
[6] Hening, I, 277, 421, 520-21, 545; II, 106. A few plantations continued their representation for a short time after 1634.—*Colonial Virginia Register,* p. 60.
[7] Hening, II, 22. Act of 1660/1.

Assembly. At the polls they were to view the returns and, before the Assembly met, to return to the secretary's office at James City the names of the persons elected "by subscription and of the major part of the hands of the electors." The penalty for a false return or neglect of duty was fixed at ten thousand pounds of tobacco.[8]

Although the writs of election were, with a very few exceptions, sent to the sheriff after 1634, between 1619 and 1634, they seem to have been directed to the commanders of the plantations. Before the advent of the sheriff his more responsible duties seem to have been performed by the commander, and the remainder by the provost-marshal. In January, 1623/4, Governor Wyatt ordered Captain William Tucker to assemble all the free men in the plantations under his command to elect by plurality of voices two burgesses.[9] An entry in the Accomac County records of 1636 points to the commander as the election official. On command of the governor and Council "for the Elexion of Burgasses out of this County," the commander, with the consent of the commissioners, ordered the inhabitants of the county to meet together at the sheriff's house, where on February 15 they assembled and chose Mr. John Howe and Mr. William Roper.[10] This incident indicates an extension into the era of the sheriff of the earlier practice.

[8] *Ibid.*, I, 411-12. Reënacted in 1657/8.
[9] Virginia Company Records, 1621-26, II, 53.
[10] Accomac County Records, 1632-40, p. 61; *Va. Mag. of Hist. and Biog.*, IV, 403.

After 1636 we find no other mention in the county records or elsewhere of the commander's performing this function, though the office continues for some years, all writs for elections hereafter going to the official most closely identified with the county—the sheriff.

In regard to the means employed in notifying the voters, a statute of 1645 provided that the sheriff inform the inhabitants of an election at least six days before the time of meeting, and by the Acts of 1654/5 and 1657/8 he was to do this from house to house throughout his county.[11] However, because of the complaints coming to the Assembly that the sheriffs had often failed to give notice of the coming elections, the house-to-house notification was abandoned in favor of the more systematic and thoroughgoing plan provided by the Act of 1661/2. Hereafter, the sheriff was to make copies of the writ of election he had received and send one to the minister of each parish in his county; the minister in turn was obliged to read the same for two successive Sundays, and return the copy with his attestation of the fact to the sheriff.[12]

Since the sheriff could compel no one to leave his plantation to vote,[13] a considerable number of freemen remained at home and voted by proxy until this was prohibited under penalty by an Act of 1646 requiring all voters to vote *viva voce* at the court-

[11] Hening, I, 411, 475.
[12] Hening, II, 82.
[13] *Ibid.*, I, 227. Act of January, 1639/40.

house.[14] For the remainder of the period the method of voting alternated between voting by plurality of voices and voting by ballot.

In 1670 a property franchise was adopted. The Assembly restricted the suffrage to freeholders and housekeepers who paid the taxes and who alone were thought entitled to vote. Bacon's Assembly, however, restored the franchise to all freemen as before 1670; this remained the law until 1684, when the right to vote was again restricted to property holders.[15]

Though the procedure in electing to the House of Burgesses was quite clearly modeled after that employed in the choice of members of the House of Commons, the units of representation were at no time identical. In Virginia certain parishes after 1634 were represented, the parish elections like the county elections being under the supervision of the sheriff; in England none of the parishes had separate representation. To correspond to the representation of many boroughs and cities in England we find, in our period, Jamestown alone represented. In the colony the number of burgesses differed among the counties. In 1619 there were two burgesses from each representative unit, but wide variations soon arose. Between 1629 and 1645 some plantations had as many as six representatives, and one county, even after 1634, had eight, while others sent only

[14] *Ibid.*, pp. 333-34.
[15] Bruce, *Inst. Hist. of Va.*, II, 415.

one.¹⁶ An Act of 1645 provided that each county have no more than four burgesses, except James City County which was to send five for the county and one for the town.¹⁷ In March, 1660/1, the number was reduced to two for each county and one for Jamestown.¹⁸

GOVERNMENTAL COMMUNICATION IN MARYLAND

In Maryland the sheriff's duties of governmental communication were about the same. The few differences existing in the election system were due to the use of the hundred in St. Mary's County for nearly two decades as the unit of representation, and to the extraordinary powers given to the commander of Kent, who, until about 1650, supervised and made returns of the elections in that part of the province in place of the sheriff.

For the organization of the courts, the execution of their orders, and the county-wide publication of proclamations and orders sent down from St. Mary's, the county and provincial governments of Maryland relied mainly on the sheriff. The varied nature of these duties and their importance in the government of Maryland are indicated by numerous examples. The sheriff was ordered to summon eleven persons to appear at a certain place and date to take the oath of commissioner and justice of the peace;¹⁹ to summon special sessions of the county court for the as-

¹⁶ J. A. C. Chandler, *Representation in Virginia*, p. 269.
¹⁷ Hening, I, 300.
¹⁸ *Ibid.*, II, 20. Reënacted in 1661/2.
¹⁹ *Proceedings of the Council, 1636-67*, pp. 348, 351.

sessing of the county poll taxes, or for the election of burgesses; to notify a justice of the peace of his dismissal;[20] to proclaim in the most public places that ordinary-keepers appear to renew their licenses;[21] and to publish in the county court, and by a note tacked on the court door, the fees which surveyors might justly take.[22] The sheriff notified the burgesses in his county to attend postponed meetings of the Assembly;[23] he proclaimed elections, the new commissioners of the peace,[24] the Protectorate, the accession of Charles II, and the succession to the proprietary rule of Charles Calvert.[25] On one occasion the Council even commanded the sheriffs to publish a proclamation against their own extortions, and the justices of the peace in each county to see that they obeyed.[26]

SIGNIFICANCE OF THE HUNDRED

The election system in Maryland deserves closer attention because of certain outstanding differences. In England the counties, boroughs, and cities were the units of representation, in Virginia after 1634, the counties, Jamestown, and a few parishes; but in St. Mary's County, Maryland, the hundred continued as the election district from the date of meeting of

[20] *Ibid., 1671-81,* p. 275.
[21] *Ibid., 1667-87/88,* p. 123; Baltemore County Records, Liber F., 1691-93, p. 240.
[22] *Proceedings of the Council, 1671-81,* p. 29.
[23] *Assembly Proceedings, 1637/8-1664,* pp. 213-14.
[24] Kent County Records, Liber A, 1654-56, p. 102.
[25] *Proceedings of the Council, 1636-67,* pp. 304, 393; Charles County Records, 1674-76, p. 172.
[26] 1678. *Proceedings of the Council, 1671-81,* pp. 201-3.

the second assembly, in January, 1637/8, until 1654 when the hundred representation was swept away by Cromwell's commissioners in favor of the county.[27] According to the election returns it was restored to St. Mary's County in March, 1657/8, but for only a short time, for the election return of 1659/60 gives the names of the burgesses for the whole county of St. Mary's and not for its several hundreds.[28] As for the counties formed after St. Mary's up to 1689 the election returns are of delegates for the counties and not for the hundreds. Soon after 1660 the hundred completely disappeared from the election system. The county had taken its place.

Who was the election official in Maryland? In St. Mary's County before 1650 there was no official to whom the writs were always addressed. The governor summoned to the Assembly of 1637/8 the members of the Council and a few other influential men. All other freemen were permitted to attend in person or to choose delegates, with the result that they chose proxies instead of delegates.[29] For the next Assembly, that of 1638/9, personal invitations were addressed to the more influential planters and writs of election to the freemen of each of the four hundreds and one manor.[30]

[27] *Assembly Proceedings, 1637/8-64,* pp. 2-6, 74-75, 88-89, 114, 127-29, 238, 260, 298, 340.
[28] *Provincial Court Proceedings, 1658-62,* pp. 61-62; *Assembly Proceedings, 1637/8-64,* pp. 383-84.
[29] N. D. Mereness, *Maryland as a Proprietary Province,* p. 195.
[30] *Assembly Proceedings 1637/8-64,* p. 27.
"After my hearty Commendations &c Whereas I have ap-

This Assembly was composed of the governor, five persons who had received a personal summons, two delegates from each of the four hundreds, and one from a manor. Up to and including 1650 the governor ordered the freemen to appear in person, by proxy, or to elect delegates. In that year and the years following, the membership of the House was constituted solely through election.[31] An Act of 1638/39, though vetoed by Lord Baltimore, indicates the subordinate place of the sheriff in the election system at that date. It was provided that the commander summon the freemen of the province to an election; on his failure to do so this duty should devolve upon the high constable of each hundred;

pointed to hold a General Assembly at St Maries on the twelfe day of ffebruary next there to advise and Consult upon the enacting of Laws and other Serious affairs of the Province, These are therefore to will and require you at Some Convenient time when you Shall think fit after the receipt of these Letters, to assemble at Kent ffort, all the freemen inhabiting within the Isle of Kent and then and there to propound to the Said ffreemen to chuse from amongst themselves two or more discreet honest men to be their deputies or Burgesses during the next assembly according to the form of an Instrument which I herewith Send unto you, to which Instrument, which I herein Send you to wch Instrument all the Said ffreemen are to set their hands, And if they agree not in the election, then you are to return upon the Instrument the names of Such two or more persons upon whome the major part of the ffreemen Soe assembled Shall consent, And you Shall require the ffreemen So assembled to agree upon a Certain Contribution for the defraying of the Charges wch Such Burgesses Shall sustain by the repairing to the assembly And together with them you Shall return hither the Instrument of their Election Signed as is appointed afore, And for Soe doeing this Shall be your warrant, Given at St Maries this 21th Decemb 1638. To my Loveing Kinsman Will: Brainthwait Commander of the—"

[31] N. D. Mereness, *op. cit.*, p. 196.

and if he did not, then should the sheriff of St. Mary's.[32] During the next few years the choice of election officials varied. In 1640 the command was specifically to "our Beloved John Robinson high Constable of Saint Clements hundred" to summon the freemen to an election of a burgess for that hundred;[33] other writs were addressed to the freemen of St. Mary's and St. George's hundreds.[34] In February, 1641/2, the sheriff of St. Mary's was ordered to assemble the freemen of four hundreds of the county, St. Mary's, St. Michael's, St. George's, and Conception or Mattapanient, at the time and place designated by him in each hundred, and the high constable of St. Clement's hundred to have like charge over the election in that hundred.[35]

As for Kent County, before 1650 the writs of election seem to have been addressed to the commander.[36] In April, 1642, the governor authorized the commander of the Isle of Kent for Kent, the sheriff of St. Mary's for all the hundreds of St. Mary's, except St. Clement's hundred, and Thomas Gerard, a planter, for that hundred, to summon the freemen within their limits to an election.[37] Beginning with 1650, that is, except during the early years of St. Mary's and Kent counties, writs of election

[32] *Assembly Proceedings, 1637/8-64,* pp. 74-75.
[33] *Ibid.,* p. 88.
[34] *Ibid.,* p. 87.
[35] *Ibid.,* p. 114-15.
[36] In 1640 to William Brainthwayte—*Assembly Proceedings, 1637/8-64,* p. 87; in 1642 to Giles Brent (p. 127); in April, 1650, to the sheriff of Kent (p. 260).
[37] *Assembly Proceedings, 1637/8-64,* p. 127.

were always addressed to the sheriffs, even to the sheriff of St. Mary's County, where the hundreds continued their representation for a few more years.[38]

On receipt of the writ from the secretary, the election official notified the voters in the "most public and convenient places" in the county. During the very early years of the colony the sheriff read the proclamation of election at the Fort of St. Mary's;[39] however, with the growth in population and division of the province into more counties, proclamation was made in the county court as the most public place in the county. The sheriff of Talbot County cried the election of 1670 in the Talbot County court in this manner: "O yes all freem of this County who have a plantacon seased of fifty acres of land at the least or a valluable p sonall Estate to the value of forty pounds starling at ye least you are to take note that you are to be at ye next Courtt to be held for this County to appeare at the house of Jona: Hopkinson being Tusday the 17th day of Jan^{r}y next by nine of the Clocke in ye morning being the day & time apoynted for the Election & Chooseing of deputies & delegates to serve for this County of Talbott in a Gen^{ll} Assembly shortly after to be Called at which time yo^u are Authorized and Required to Elect & Choose foure seaverell & sufficient ffreemen each of them haveing a sufficient vissible estate a plantacon seated of fifty acres of land at the least or a vissible

---

[38] *Ibid.*, pp. 259-60, 298, 369; *Provincial Court Proceedings, 1658-62*, pp. 61-62; *William and Mary Coll. Quart.*, V, 49; Kent County Records, 1657-62, pp. 200-1.

[39] *Assembly Proceedings 1637/8-64*, pp. 115-16.

p sonall estate at lest forty pounds starling with this county. God save the Lord Proprietary."[40] Those not present at court were notified individually by the constables of their hundreds.[41]

The election official was sometimes authorized by the governor to select the date and place of election;[42] the writ of election of 1660/1 even gave the sheriff authority to determine the number to be chosen.[43] In the early years of St. Mary's the polling place was often a planter's home. The freemen of St. Mary's hundred in the election of 1642 were ordered by the governor to assemble before the sheriff of St. Mary's "at some place near the fort" on the afternoon of Saturday, July 9; those of St. Michael's hundred at whatever place the sheriff appointed in that hundred, on July 16; and those of St. George's hundred before David Wickliff, planter, at his home, on July 9.[44]

The hundreds remained the polling places until supplanted by the counties as electoral districts. It was Dr. Wilhelm's belief that the hundreds continued as the polling places even after the abolition of the hundred representation, but the records show beyond a doubt that by 1670 the delegates were being elected in the county courts.[45] In case the next meeting of

[40] Talbot County Records, Liber B. B., 1662-73, p. 158.
[41] *Ibid.*
[42] *Assembly Proceedings, 1637/8-64,* pp. 88, 114, 115, 127.
[43] *Ibid.,* p. 395.
[44] *Ibid.,* pp. 127-28.
[45] L. W. Wilhelm, *Local Institutions of Maryland,* pp. 349, 376; *Proceedings of the Council, 1667-87/8,* pp, 77-78; Kent County Records, 1676-95, pp. 61, 235^2; Talbot County Records, Liber B. B., 1662-73, p. 158; Baltimore County Records, Liber F., 1691-93, p. 170.

the county court after the sheriff's proclamation came so late as to delay the election returns to the secretary beyond the date of meeting of the Assembly, the sheriff was directed to call the county court into special session.[46]

Soon after the county became the unit of representation, elections came as completely under the sheriff's charge in Maryland as they were during the period in England and in Virginia after 1634. The writs of election were addressed to the sheriffs; they proclaimed the election in the county court and in other public places; they supervised the voting in the county court and returned to the chancellor and the governor indentures of election, containing the time and place of election, the names of the delegates chosen, and the signatures of the sheriff and the voters.[47] The sheriff also notified those elected to appear at St. Mary's by the date named in the writ.

COMPARISON WITH ENGLAND

The foregoing descriptions of the election systems of Virginia and Maryland show the widest divergences from the English system to have occurred during the period preceding the full development of their county governments. In Virginia before 1634 the commanders of the plantations seem to have been the election officials and not the provost-marshals; in the Isle of Kent, the later Kent County, Maryland, for over a decade the commander had charge of elec-

[46] Kent County Records, 1676-95, p. 61; Baltemore County Records, Liber F., 1691-93, p. 170.
[47] *Proceedings of the Council, 1667-87/8*, pp. 77-78.

tions and not the sheriff, and in St. Mary's County the use of the hundred as the sole election district gave to the freemen and constables of the hundreds for a time the election duties later required of the sheriffs.

In regard to the conduct of the sheriffs while executing their election duties, there are not a few charges of misconduct and negligence[48]—there were, as we have noticed, many complaints against the English sheriff—but how great was the extent of their misdeeds, alone, or in comparison with those of the English sheriffs, cannot be very well estimated from the records.

[48] Hening, I, 532, 545; II, 33, 82. *Assembly Proceedings, 1666-67,* pp. 74, 187; *Proceedings of the Council, 1667-87/8,* p. 149.

Chapter IX

FINANCIAL DUTIES

Collector of Poll Taxes

THE FINANCIAL duties of the sheriff were considerably more important in Virginia than in England. In the colony he was responsible for the collection not only of the royal revenues, but also of the most productive of the colonial revenues—the poll taxes. His work as a strictly colonial official in the assessment and collection of the public, county, and parish poll taxes, was one of his outstanding functions.

During the first half of the period under survey the Assembly experimented with several different methods of drawing up the lists of the tithables, those who paid the poll taxes. For a time this responsibility was given alternately to the sheriffs and to commissioners by appointment of the county court. The commissioners were nearly always from the bench and therefore self-appointed.[1] A statute of 1657/8 provided for the unique plan of having the heads of families make out lists of their tithables and present them during the month of June to the clerk of the county court to be recorded,[2] but when the householders were found to be untrustworthy, the Assembly in March, 1658/9, again appointed the sheriffs to take the lists.[3] However, after a short

---

[1] Hening, I, 376. *William and Mary Coll. Quart.*, XXII, 241; Northampton County Records, 1645-51, p. 44; 1654-55, p. 109; Lower Norfolk County Records, 1646-51, p. 40.
[2] Hening, I, 454.
[3] *Ibid.*, p. 521.

trial, many of the sheriffs proved dishonest, causing the Assembly to give their work again to commissioners, and the commissioners continued to take the lists until the end of the period.[4]

METHOD OF TAXATION

The Act of 1661/2 provided for a systematic census taking. The county was to be divided into precincts. In each precinct the county court was to appoint a commissioner, who was to give notice on the church door of the days before June 10 on which he would receive the lists. Each commissioner was required by the Act to present to the clerk at the August term of the county court the account taken by him, with the lists handed in by the family heads, and the county clerk, in turn, was to forward to the clerk of the Assembly by the second day of the September General Court an exact list of tithables.[5] The lists submitted by the householders were also posted on the court door where omissions of any of the tithables might be discovered by the other taxpayers.[6] In 1676 we find certain counties complaining that the lists of tithables were incomplete, and suggesting as remedies that the lists be handed in under oath, and also that the clerk produce on demand the lists of tithables.[7]

[4] Acts of March, 1660/1, and March, 1661/2.
[5] Hening, II, 83-84; Northumberland County Records, 1678-98, p. 193. The constables assisted the justices both in notifying the householders and in taking the lists.—Lower Norfolk County Records, 1651-56, p. 103; York County Records, 1657-62, pp. 119, 162; Charles City County Records, 1655-65, p. 267.
[6] Hartwell, Chilton, and Blair, *Present State of Virginia, 1697-98*, sec. IX.
[7] *Va. Mag. of Hist. and Biog.*, III, 38; II, 289.

The three levies, the public, county, and parish, were apportioned by the Assembly, county court, and vestry respectively in the same manner, by dividing the whole number of tithables into the total amount of the bills owed. The public and county taxes, while kept separate in account, were collected together unless the House was late in sending its assessment to the county courts. On such occasions the justices, who met to apportion the county levy either in the October or November term, and sometimes in December, prorated and ordered the county levy collected, without waiting for the public assessment.[8]

Before 1647 the county court usually appointed the sheriff to collect the public and county levies,[9] but a General Assembly in November of that year found "great defects" in the collection of the public levies either because of the great size of the counties, "the multitude of other employments of the sherriffs," or for some other cause, and appointed in their place special collectors in each county.[10] Such was the practice in England where Parliament appointed commissioners, and not the sheriffs, to collect the taxes.

In the year following, the Assembly declared the work of the collectors to have been so superior to that of the sheriffs that the new method would be continued. The Assembly appointed the collectors

---

[8] See Henrico County Records, 1682-1701, pp. 115-16.

[9] Accomac County Records, 1640-45, p. 111; Lower Norfolk County Records, 1637-42, p. 51^2; 1645-46, p. 7; 1646-51, pp. 7-8.

[10] Hening, I, 342-43; *William and Mary Coll. Quart.*, XXIII, 273.

for Northampton and Elizabeth counties, but seems to have given to the county courts the right of appointment in the other counties.[11] For several years after 1648 the commissioners of the county courts, after prorating the county levy, assigned a collector to each precinct in the county to collect both the public and the county levies, at a fee of 10 per cent of the amount collected. They were usually members of the county bench and therefore self-appointed.[12]

A permanent system came into effect about 1654. From that year the records of most of the counties show that the commissioners, or justices, appointed the sheriff to gather the taxes. Apparently, only in Lancaster and Middlesex counties did any irregularities occur. In Lancaster during some years the members of the court appointed the sheriff to collect the taxes; at other times they appointed themselves; and during the later years of the period they appointed two persons to this duty, the sheriff for one-half of the county and generally a justice of the peace for the other half. The fee of the collector in all the counties was 10 per cent of his collections.[13]

[11] Hening, I, 356.
[12] Lower Norfolk County Records, 1646-51, pp. 128-29, 199-200; 1656-66, pp. 326-33; Northampton County Records, 1645-51, p. 156; Lancaster County Records, 1652-57, pp. 174-78. Between 1645 and 1648 the poll tax was supplanted by a tax on all the visible forms of property.
[13] See Bacon's *Laws* and Act of February, 1676/7 in Hening; Lancaster County Records, 1652-57, pp. 174-78, 234-39; 1655-66, p. 236; orders of July 11, 1677, and Dec. 14, 1678; Middlesex County Records, 1673-80, p. 88². Very early in the period the sheriff's salary is given as 5 per cent of the amount collected.—*Va. Mag. of Hist. and Biog.*, XXIII, 240, 242-43.

Since the justices were legally responsible for the levies of which the sheriffs in nearly all the counties were collectors, it was enacted that only a member of the commission who should give good security to the other justices before he took the oath of office might be sheriff of the county.[14] Thus, for greater financial security, a small group of men were given practically a monopoly over one of the most important of the county offices.

As for the parish levies, these at first were collected by the churchwardens.[15] Since the parish levies were due at the time of the public and county levies, it was found more convenient to have the sheriff collect all three together. This became the practice soon after 1660.[16]

In event of the death of the sheriff before the collection of all the levies charged to him, the county court appointed for completion of this work either his under-sheriff or certain from their own number.[17] The remainder of the duties of the collector, whether sheriff or commissioner, consisted in paying the various creditors and then appearing in the

[14] Act of 1661/2.
[15] Hening, I, 478-79; Northumberland County Records, 1652-65, p. 40^2; Lower Norfolk County Records, 1666-75, p. 67.
[16] Surry County Records, 1671-90, pp. 14, 38; Northumberland County Records, 1678-98, p. 52; St. Peter's Parish, New Kent County Vestry Book, 1685-1758, p. 20 (photostat copy, Va. State Library); Charles City County Records, 1655-65, p. 349, etc.
[17] Northampton County Records, 1664-74, pp. 95, 96; Lower Norfolk County Records, court of Feb. 17, 1678/9, and of Oct. 15, 1679.

FINANCIAL DUTIES

county court to present his account to the justices and receive his discharge.[18]

COLLECTOR'S FEES

The collector's fee was so remunerative that the question arises why the justices did not continue to divide the county among themselves for collection as they had done for a time. York County, for example, in 1658 paid its sheriff 3,159 pounds of tobacco for his collections.[19] There were, of course, those exceptions to the rule already mentioned, in Lancaster, where the justices frequently appointed themselves collectors, and in Middlesex County, to whose justices Jeffreys in 1671 addressed a letter requesting them not to take away the collection of the public levies from Captain Whitaker, their sheriff, but "to lett the Collection runn in its proper Chanell."[20] Though, according to the law, each justice of the peace should have his turn at being sheriff, some, as we have noticed, were privileged to enjoy the substantial income of the office out of their turn. The large commission received for collecting the three poll taxes contributed much to the desirability of the office; if divided among six or more justices, each would have had for his extra work but a moderate though not to be despised fee, while one of their number as sheriff would have lost his principal income. In this connection the traditional at-

[18] York County Records, 1638-48, p. 359; Charles City County Records, 1655-65, pp. 250, 351, 547, etc.
[19] York County Records, 1657-62, p. 37.
[20] Middlesex County Records, 1673-80, p. 88.

titude of regarding the office as a recourse for those who had suffered financial reverses is also to be recalled.[21]

Another form of revenue entrusted at times to the sheriff's collection was the fort or castle duty.[22] The sheriff was also responsible for the collection of the fees of the secretary and of the county clerks, of which he received 10 per cent,[23] and of the arrears in fees of the preceding sheriff. He likewise collected all court fines.[24]

Collector of King's Revenues

As collector of the King's revenues[25] the sheriff's most important obligation was the quit-rents, a feudal payment of one shilling for each fifty acres of land held of the King. In this connection he was "his majestie's imediate officer" in every county.[26]

During the early years of royal government little seems to have been accomplished toward the collection of the quit-rents, and consequently we hear much less about them. In 1640 the General Court, on motion of Roger Wingate, Treasurer, ordered the sheriffs to collect the quit-rents according to the

[21] See *supra,* Chap. VI on *Qualifications and Appointment,* note 41.

[22] Hening, I, 533-34; Lower Norfolk County Records, court order of Nov. 26, 1677.

[23] Hening, II, 26-27, 143-44.

[24] Hening, II, 66-67.

[25] Consult the sheriff's oath of office, *infra,* pp. 167-68, Illustrative Document, No. 5.

[26] Hening, II, 83.

treasurer's directions, and account to him at the next Quarter Court.[27] The method of collecting and of accounting for the King's rents is given in the governor's directions to the sheriff of York in 1685. The sheriff of York was commanded to collect one year's rent in money or tobacco, and to be guided in his collections by the patents and deeds of the landholders. The rents collected and properly receipted he should pay in at the February General Court to the auditor, and at the April court present a "full and perfect rent roll" of all lands held of the King in York County together with the receipts for all the rents he had paid in to the auditor.[28] Then his account might be checked up and his discharge issued. The sheriff was guided in his collections by past rent rolls and by the best information he could obtain of lands lately taken up.[29] His fee was 10 per cent of his collections.

Another royal revenue was derived from the forfeited estates and goods of felons. The sheriff's duties respecting forfeitures are indicated in the order of the Northampton County court of April, 1650, to the sheriff to take an inventory of the estate of his prisoner that he might seize it for the King in case he were convicted of murder.[30]

In regard to the collection of the rather indefinite

[27] *Va. Mag. of Hist. and Biog.*, V, 365.

[28] York County Records, 1684-87, pp. 127-28; *see also* Colonial Office, Class 5, vol. 1405, p. 141. Printed in *Executive Journals of the Council of Colonial Virginia*, I, 202.

[29] Hartwell, Chilton, and Blair, *Present State of Virginia, 1697-98*, sec. IX.

[30] Northampton County Records, 1645-51, p. 209².

series of other royal revenues for which the English sheriff was responsible, like wreck of the sea, treasure trove, etc., the records are not altogether silent. The sheriff and coroners were ordered to seize and to account to the governor from time to time for all wrecks, waifs, strays, felons' goods, etc., found within their counties.[31] There is no phase of colonial finance more absorbing than the casual revenues, and no study so much neglected as this mediaeval survival lingering on in the New World.

Deodands

An interesting form of revenue collectible by the sheriff and not infrequently met with in the court records, was deodands. From very early times it had been the custom in England for the sheriff to seize for the King, where the deodand belonged to the King, anything which had by accident caused the death of a person. The thing seized was then sold and given to charity, that is, to God. In Charles City County a coroner's jury found that George Bollington had died as a result of an accidental fall from his horse, and they declared the horse deodand.[32] An inquest before Richard Conquest, sheriff of Lower Norfolk in 1646, found the death of Nathaniel Kingsland due to the turning over of the boat he was in and declared the attachment of the boat "in regard it was the Cause of his death, and

---

[31] Colonial Office, Class 5, vol. 1405, p. 268. Printed in *Executive Journals of the Council of Colonial Virginia*, II, 86-87, and *infra*, Illustrative Documents, No. 23.

[32] Charles City County Records, 1655-66, pp. 515, 519.

is appraysed to ye value of one hundred pounds of tob. and remaynes in ye Custody of the said sherriffe."³³

TAX COLLECTOR IN MARYLAND

When we examine the financial duties of the sheriff in Maryland we find few important variations. Like the Virginia sheriff he was responsible for the collection of the poll taxes, and of the proprietary, in place of the royal, revenues.

While in Virginia the lists of tithables were taken by the sheriffs for a few years only and during the rest of the time by commissioners, who were usually justices, in Maryland this work seems always to have belonged to the sheriff. To his patent of office was attached a warrant authorizing him to take a list of all the tithables in his county, the list to contain the name of each tithable, with his place of residence, and to be completed by a date set, often the twentieth of July. After taking the lists the sheriffs were to make two exact copies, one to be sent to the governor and Council, and the other to be tacked up in the courthouse at the next county court for the public view and correction of errors.³⁴ All householders were thus given an opportunity to expose the cheating of a neighbor and save themselves from being overcharged. In addition, the lists were supposed to

---

[33] The names of the sheriff and the six jurors follow—Lower Norfolk County Records, 1646-51, pp. 89-90; see also *ibid.*, p. 116².

[34] *Proceedings of the Council, 1636-67,* pp. 456-57, 492-93; *1667-87/8,* p. 3; Somerset Connty Records, Liber B 1, 1665-68, p. 24.

be carefully examined by the justices of the peace and any mistakes rectified before being used by the Assembly and county court as the basis for making up the public and county levies.[35]

As the lists were taken by hundreds most of the actual work of visiting each household and enquiring of its head the number of his or her tithables fell to the constables of the hundreds, who on the completion of their task handed in their lists to the sheriff.[36]

On the basis of the sheriff's report of the number of tithables in his county, the public levy was assessed by a tax commission assembled at St. Mary's Town, composed of one or more persons from each hundred, or from each county not yet divided into hundreds.[37] In 1649 the Assembly ordered the governor to issue writs to the sheriff of St. Mary's County to summon an election in each hundred of two persons to assess the taxes for the hundreds.[38] For almost two decades the taking of the lists of tithables and the assessment of the poll taxes in St. Mary's County were purely hundred affairs.

The amount of the public levy was sent down from St. Mary's to the county, apparently to the sheriff when the justices were not in court, to be collected with the county levy. In case the next county court was not to meet until long after the arrival of the public assessment, the sheriff was directed by the

[35] *Proceedings of the Council, 1671-81,* p. 156.
[36] *Assembly Proceedings, 1666-76,* pp. 538-39.
[37] Wilhelm, *Local Institutions of Maryland,* pp. 350-51.
[38] *Assembly Proceedings, 1637/8-1664,* p. 238.

governor to call several justices into a special meeting and thus prevent any financial inconvenience to the public and county creditors.[39] The items making up the county levy were those found in the Virginia lists: rewards for wolves' heads, the coroner's, the crier's, and the doorkeeper's salaries, the fees of those attending the burgesses to St. Mary's, the expenses of the burgesses, the expenses of the justices in laying the levy, the sheriff's fees for his prisoners, the secretary's fee for a copy of the laws, etc.[40] The sheriff received 10 per cent of his collections. His duties were ended after paying to each creditor the amount due him.

From these general remarks on the method of taking the lists of tithables and of assessing and collecting the poll taxes, it is obvious that the system employed in Maryland was quite similar to that in use in Virginia. In fact, they correspond so closely in most respects as to suggest that Maryland copied from the older colony. Two differences have been noticed: the use of the hundred in Maryland instead of the precinct as the census and assessment unit, and the taking of the lists of tithables by the sheriff instead of by commissioners, for which Virginia during several years of the period furnished a precedent.

Proprietary Revenues

The proprietary revenues consisted of most of the royal revenues, with certain additional land pay-

[39] Somerset County Records, Liber B 1, 1665-68, p. 125.
[40] Talbot County Records, Liber B B, pp. 12, 157; Dorchester County Records, 1689-92, November court, 1690; Kent County Records, 1676-95, p. 251.

ments. The sheriff was required by his commission to collect the Proprietor's rents, revenues, fines, forfeitures, and "all other profitt, & p quisits whatsoever," and to have 10 per cent of such receipts.[41]

Quit-rents were the most valuable of all the revenues belonging to the Proprietor. They were collected by the sheriff according to the rent roll which he made up, and which with the assistance of the county clerk he was expected to keep up to date.[42] The rents were brought in by the tenants to the sheriff's house or to whatever places he designated.[43] The sheriff accounted for the quit-rents to the receiver-general.

Of the other land revenues, caution or purchase money and composition money were due when the tenant purchased his land from the Proprietor. Composition money was paid when the warrant was taken out.[44] Alienation fines are found recorded among the deeds in the county land records. They were feudal dues of one year's rent payable to the Proprietor's representative in the county, the sheriff, on alienation of land by one tenant to another.[45]

Besides collecting the revenues accruing to the Proprietor from his lands, the sheriff acted in the

---

[41] *Proceedings of the Council 1636-67*, p. 147.
[42] *Ibid., 1667-87/8*, pp. 70, 91-92; *1671-81*, p. 159.
[43] *Ibid., 1636-67*, p. 458.
[44] Wilhelm, *Local Institutions of Maryland*, pp. 328 f.
[45] It is recorded in the Charles County Records, 1665-68, that Jeremiah Dickenson acknowledged and paid to the sheriff a year's rent as a due to the Lord Proprietor for the alienation of 300 acres of land to him by William Allen (p. 84). For other examples of alienation fines, see Somerset County Records, Liber W. W., 1676-79, pp. 8-9, 166, 211.

capacity of escheator by taking possession of all lands that had escheated to the Proprietor. He was required to furnish a detailed description of such lands to the receiver-general.[46]

The sheriff also collected for the Proprietor all court fines and forfeitures for which he also accounted to the receiver-general. The following itemized list contains the various revenues with their amounts for which the province in 1673 sued Stephen Tully, sheriff of Talbot County the year preceding. The sum of the revenues totaled 44,850 pounds of tobacco; of this amount Tully was given credit for only 5,521 pounds:

To rents of the county	17433
To the secretary's fees	12736
To fines and amercements	01650
To alienations	01156
To tobacco received of Mr. Hemsley	02000
To tobacco received of Mr. Ward	01500

and more items like the last two above, which were probably poll taxes.[47]

Still another revenue which the sheriff collected for the Proprietor, though not for his personal use, deodands,[48] has already been sufficiently discussed under the financial duties of the Virginia sheriff.

THE SHERIFF'S ACCOUNTING

We have thus far described the duties of the sheriff in collecting poll taxes, certain royal and propri-

[46] *Proceedings of the Council, 1667-87/8*, p. 122; *Provincial Court Proceedings*, Liber M. M., 1672-75, p. 32.
[47] *Ibid.*, p. 444.
[48] *Ibid., 1637-50*, pp. 9-10.

etary revenues, and deodands. We are given none of the details of the accounting at Jamestown and at St. Mary's, merely the general statement in Ludwell's letter to Arlington to the effect that the sheriff and other collectors appeared at Jamestown twice a year before the auditor-general and took out their discharge from him "as out of the Exchequer in England."[49] This statement naturally causes us to wonder whether or not the sheriff was troubled with any of the numerous technicalities and expenses which burdened the English sheriff when accounting into the Exchequer and helped to make his office undesirable to most men. The judicial system and court procedure of England were greatly simplified to meet the pressing needs of the colonists, and it is quite unlikely that much delay or expense was permitted in the process of accounting at Jamestown and St. Mary's.

Comparison with England

One important difference between the financial duties of the colonial sheriff and those of the English sheriff has been noted: the English sheriff accounted for the royal revenues in his county, but parliamentary taxes were collected by commissioners appointed by Parliament or by the higher government officials; the colonial sheriff collected not only royal or proprietary revenues but, in addition, the poll taxes. He was both a royal, or proprietary, and a colonial officer. What was the probable reason for this differ-

[49] *Va. Mag. of Hist. and Biog.*, V, 59.

ence, which is more evident in Virginia? Parliament may have thought that in England the added responsibility of tax-collecting would overburden the office. At one time in Virginia this was the reason assigned for taking this duty from the sheriff and giving it to commissioners, and yet within a few years the sheriff was again appointed collector, though the burden of his duties could not have been lessened. Virginia tried for a time the English method of appointing commissioners, or special collectors, to collect the levies, but eventually supplanted these officers in nearly all the counties with the sheriff. This permanent change, however, was not made because the sheriff was found to be more efficient and honest in collecting than the commissioners. Most probably Parliament did not appoint the sheriff to collect its taxes through fear of the King. This was the period in England of the struggle between King and Parliament for supremacy; such addition to the sheriff's financial duties would have greatly increased the royal power. The colonial justices had less to fear. They could more safely entrust the sheriff with the responsibility of collecting the taxes because of the greater independence he possessed in Virginia. He was much freer of royal control than the English sheriff; he was far more responsible to the members of his own social and political group in the county, by whom he was nominated and often virtually elected. If, after the Restoration, much of this local independence of action had been taken away, had Berkeley, for example, been able to appoint the sheriffs and under-sheriffs regularly without consulting the wishes of the justices of the peace, the planters would, no doubt, have taken from the sheriff the collection of the poll taxes, and the English system would have been adopted. As a consequence, the power and usefulness of the sheriff in the colonies would have been greatly reduced.

Chapter X

CONSERVATOR OF THE PEACE: CONCLUSION

POLICE POWERS

THE POLICE powers of the colonial sheriff remain to be discussed. He was the principal keeper of the peace in Virginia and, as in England, had the legal authority to command in an emergency all able-bodied persons with their arms, horses, and boats. The *posse comitatus* was at his disposal then as it is today. The Stafford justices, for example, after ordering the imprisonment of a certain person for abusing the governor and themselves, proclaimed in open court that all persons on command assist the sheriff or his deputy.[1] A Lancaster County court in 1653 authorized the sheriff "to raise such power as may be sufficient" for the prevention of a duel in that county.[2] When it was testified before one of the early quarter courts that although the provost-marshal called upon all the bystanders in the name of the King to help him put a disorderly fellow in the stocks, one of their number had walked away laughing, the judges fined the culprit forty pounds of tobacco for disobedience to orders.[3]

The raising of hue and cry is seldom mentioned in

---

[1] Stafford County Records, 1664-68, p. 67.
[2] Lancaster County Records, 1652-57, p. 65. Printed in *Va. Mag. of Hist. and Biog.*, II, 97.
[3] 1628. *Ibid.*, XXXI, 149.

the records.[4] It was probably little resorted to in Virginia because of the wide scattering of the population.

Enforcing Political Conformity

The sheriff and the justices were to warn, and if the occasion warranted, disperse or seize all rioters. As in England reports on disorderly gatherings were handed in to the courts signed by the sheriff and at least two justices of the peace. One of these reports, appearing in the records of Lower Norfolk County, is of a seditious meeting in the Church of Elizabeth River Parish in 1648, which the sheriff, Richard Conquest, ordered to disperse in these words: "All manner of persons here mett and assembled are in the Kings Ma^{ts} name strictly required and commanded, forthwith and immediately to retorne to their severall dwellings, or habitations, as they or any of them, will answer theire contempts to the contrary at their uttermost perills."[5] Not to multiply illustrations, the sheriff of Surry in 1673 was commanded by the justices to take into custody certain members of a disorderly crowd which had collected for the purpose of altering or not paying the levy;[6] and the sheriff of Northampton in 1651 was ordered to take prisoners fifty men who, without authority, had attacked the Indians and caused them to gather for an attack on the county.[7]

[4] Hening, II, 282; York County Records, 1664-72, p. 226.
[5] Lower Norfolk County Records, 1646-51, pp. 74-75.
[6] Surry County Records, 1671-84, p. 42.
[7] Northampton County Records, 1651-54, p. 40.

Enforcing Religious Conformity

The colony in its attempts toward the enforcement of religious conformity relied much on the sheriff to discover and present nonconformists. As regards the Puritans we learn that Richard Conquest, sheriff of Lower Norfolk in 1649, presented to the county court the names of eight persons, two of them commissioners, and of certain others, who though above sixteen years of age had nevertheless, contrary to the Elizabethan statute, remained away from their church for three months and had refused to hear read the Book of Common Prayer. The justices had the prisoners give bond to appear at Jamestown by a certain date to answer the sheriff's charges.[8]

The Quakers were to be closely watched by the sheriff and justices, especially after Berkeley's return to Virginia. By a statute of 1659/60 all Quakers were to be apprehended and imprisoned without bail until they left the colony or put in security to leave.[9] The York County court, in an effort to prevent more meetings of Quakers and to preserve the peace, which they considered mostly the same thing, ordered the high sheriff and the other county officials to search out their unlawful assemblies and warn against further meetings.[10] Berkeley, hearing that the sheriff of Lower Norfolk in 1660, Richard Conquest, was altogether remiss in "not stopping yee frequent meetings of this most pestilent Sect of ye quakers"

[8] Lower Norfolk County Records, 1646-51, p. 121.
[9] Hening, I, 532-33.
[10] York County Records, 1657-62, p. 63.

charged him strictly to suffer no more of their meetings.[11] After this date there are numerous reports of the sheriff's efforts to suppress this sect. They presented to the courts the names of those taken in meeting and the name of the owner of the house that harboured them; they levied the fines imposed, one-half of which went to the informer and the other half to the public.[12]

A greater animosity was displayed in Virginia toward the Roman Catholics, both in the statutes and in the popular attitude, though the records lack information on the sheriff's activity toward their discovery and seizure.

The county prison was under the sheriff's charge. The Assembly passed many laws ordering strong prisons to be built in each county after the form of a Virginia house, and making the county liable to the sheriff for escape from any other kind. Many sheriffs, in accordance with these acts, immediately after their appointment petitioned the justices to execute the law, but the century was far advanced before the counties built regulation prisons and abandoned the makeshift rooms and houses they had been using. Several counties used one or two rooms in the sheriff's house; in one county a room in the house where the court met was set aside for this purpose.[13]

[11] *William and Mary Coll. Quart.*, II, 172.

[12] Hening, II, 198; *Lower Norfolk County Virginia Antiquary*, III, 141-46; Lower Norfolk County Records, 1656-66, pp. 302, 374².

[13] Lower Norfolk County Records, 1656-66, p. 206; Accomac County Records, 1666-70, p. 30; Stafford County Records, 1664-68, p. 20.

The Stafford court in 1665 ordered that "the Little house ags^t. the Court house" be fitted for a prison, while the justices of York in 1662 expecting the next levy to be high and hoping at the same time that the Assembly would accept this as a sufficient excuse, gave orders that the sheriff's house be the county prison.[14]

It is obvious that the maintenance of political and religious conformity and of general good order throughout Virginia was largely in the sheriff's hands. In Maryland his authority was fully as great.[15]

General Summary

This comparative study proves the similarities in the office of sheriff in England and in her colonies to have been decidedly more numerous than the differences. In both countries the office was occupied by representatives from closely resembling social and economic groups, and appointment was made in much the same manner. The colonial office was more sought after because it always assured its occupant a substantial income. His fees were good even when not supplemented with those of the coroner, clerk, or surveyor, whose offices he sometimes added to his own. He was, besides, free of the great official expenses incurred by the English sheriff while accounting into the Exchequer and entertaining at

[14] York County Records, 1657-62, p. 182.
[15] *Proceedings of the Council, 1671-81,* pp. 247-48, 377; *Provincial Court Proceedings, 1637-50,* p. 241; *Assembly Proceedings, 1666-76,* pp. 223-24.

the assizes. With a few exceptions, the general nature of their duties was alike. The colonial sheriff published proclamations, supervised and returned elections, executed the administrative and judicial business of the courts, kept the peace, and collected the royal and proprietary revenues, performing these ancient duties of the English office in most respects with close conformity to English law and custom. He lacked the few small judicial functions of the English sheriff; in Maryland he was deprived for a time of his election duties, and in both Virginia and Maryland he was largely free of ceremonial duties. On the other hand, he had, in the colonies, a far greater importance as a financial officer than in England, by reason of the fact that in addition to the royal and proprietary revenues he also collected the poll taxes.

Divergencies from England

The English shrievalty was not completely made over by adaptation to the environment in Virginia and Maryland; in most fundamentals it remained conspicuously English throughout the seventeenth century. Yet the comparatively few divergencies that arose were important. They mark a line of development, an additional importance, that was not later realized in England. A study of the causes of these divergencies reveals the powerful influence exerted by the newness of the environment upon the remolding of this ancient institution, in the process of which most of its devitalized and undemocratic parts were cast aside, while other parts were reinvigorated with some of their early strength. A few small duties of a financial nature survived in the colonies, the collecting of deodands and of certain royal and proprietary revenues. Quit-rents, however, had too important a place in colonial life to be considered as simply another mediaeval survival lingering on in the free atmosphere of the New World. The only aristocratic characteristic of the office that we can be sure survived was its exclusive control by the group of larger landowners in each county. But to this end the environment in the colonies was as favorable as it was in England.

The more pronounced divergencies in the colonies group themselves under six heads: the increase in financial powers; the lack of judicial functions; the temporary loss of election duties; the more purely local than royal and provincial character of the office; the more democratic character of the office; and its more important place in colonial county government. As we have already discussed the increase in financial powers[16] we may consider first the second point, the non-judicial character of the colonial office, and then the other differences that have been enumerated.

Lack of Judicial Functions

The sheriff's court duties comprised most of his work. In the main they corresponded to those of the English sheriff. The outstanding differences

[16] See *supra,* p. 144.

were due entirely to his surroundings. In no other particular is the molding energy of the economic and cultural environment more evident than in the organization and functioning of the colonial judiciary. The English judicial system, even if well understood by anyone in the colony and transplanted, could never have worked. Even had the expense of its maintenance not been too great, such a variety of courts with their overlapping jurisdictions and almost infinitely complex procedures could not have been sufficiently reformed to meet the needs of the busy inhabitants for quick and certain justice and for a kind of procedure that could be understood by the average person. No attempt was made to transplant the English judiciary, and as a consequence the colonial sheriff lacked two of the oldest and most obscure duties performed by the sheriff in England: the holding of his county court and of his tourn, or turn. Neither of these courts was brought over to the New World; with their loss went those few judicial powers still remaining to the sheriff in England, immediate in the tourn, and indirect in the county court through the opportunities offered for influencing court decisions. The court procedure in the colonies, by reason of the prevailing ignorance of English procedure and because of the need for greater speed and less confusion, was altered so as to be almost unrecognizable to an English lawyer, but it was thereby far better understood by the judges, attorneys, and others attending court, and decidedly more workable under pioneer conditions.

Election Divergencies

Concerning election duties, the plan of election in both colonies was clearly an adaptation of the English election system. The resemblance was most marked when the county government was furthest developed. At that time the sheriff proclaimed, supervised, and returned elections with a responsibility fully equal to that of the English sheriff. The noteworthy divergencies in Virginia were developed between 1619 and 1634, with the establishment of civil government and before the formation of counties. In this period the hundreds and boroughs, ill defined groups of settlements, became the election units, and the commander the election official. This irregular arrangement was not intended to be permanent and was entirely swept away within a few years after the counties were established; nevertheless it formed the model for the election system in Maryland for more than a decade. In St. Mary's County the hundred was made the election unit, and, as a consequence, either the freemen or constables performed for a limited time, less than one-third of the entire period, the election duties of their hundreds. Hundred representation was without precedent in English history. In the early 1650's the sheriff, a county official, returned the election in each hundred of St. Mary's County; for this anomalous arrangement a precedent is not to be found in either Virginia or England. It was one of those irregularities in Maryland local government that later passed away with the development of the county at the expense of the hundred. Another borrowing from Virginia is indicated in the employment of the commander until about 1650 as the election official of Kent County.

COLONIAL COUNTY MORE INDEPENDENT

Another point of divergence lies in the fact that, though appointed by the governor, the colonial sheriff belonged more to the county than to the central government. He was more of a county than a colonial official, and this seems to have been due to the absence of such close relations as existed between the central and local governments in England. The English connecting links were either not present in the colonies or, when present, were not nearly so strong. The colonial governments devised, in this early period, nothing comparable to the English system of circuit courts for supervising the administration of the county. Members of the council sat in the county courts, and circuits were established in Virginia by a statute of 1661/2, but the hardships of traveling, the loss of time to the councillors, and the increased expense to the counties caused their early abandonment.[17] Had they been continued the planters would probably have been too jealous of their rights to suffer without complaint much supervision from without. As a connecting link, the sheriff was called upon less often for the administration of colonial affairs for the reason that there was much less colonial business administered in the counties. For these and perhaps other reasons the counties main-

[17] Bruce, *Inst. Hist. of Va.*, I, 499.

tained throughout most of the period a considerably greater degree of independence in ordering their affairs than was enjoyed by the English counties. County self-government did not exist at any time in seventeenth-century England; in the colonies it became a reality early in the century.

Sheriff More Independent

Furthermore, as a member of the ruling group in the county the sheriff shared its independence. This has been observed throughout the process of his appointment and induction into office, and also in the fact that by far the greater part of his duties originated in the county, for whose performance he was immediately responsible to the justices. In the matter of appointment the governor had the legal right to set aside the lists nominated by the justices and make his choice independently, but except during a part of Berkeley's second administration he seems rarely to have exercised this power. In filling vacancies, also, the governor usually appointed the nominee of the justices. In the execution of his duties the sheriff's independence of Jamestown and St. Mary's is best observed in the collection of the poll taxes: the Assembly gave to the justices the responsibility of collecting the public and county levies and they appointed whomever they pleased to the work, in most instances the sheriff, who accounted to the justices for his collections and their disbursement.

Sheriff More Democratic: More Important

The sheriff's duties in the colonies were more democratic than in England. In both countries he came from the same social and economic group as the justices of the peace, with whom he was closely associated in county administration. There is no evidence to indicate that the English sheriff, under ordinary circumstances, enjoyed any official preëminence over the justices; but on state occasions when the judges of assize, the King, or foreign ambassadors visited the county he as the county head and representative played host with full-blown ceremonial and lavish entertainment. Occasions of this sort must have been rare in the colonies, and it is doubtful if the sheriff ever imitated appreciably such display. Nevertheless, there is no doubt at all but that in both Virginia and Maryland he was looked upon as the county head. We have already noted the order to the sheriff from the governor and Council that for the proclaiming of William and Mary at Jamestown he summon the best appearance that could be had for testifying due honor and obedience and acclamations of joy, by firing of cannons, sounding of trumpets, and beating of drums. In Maryland we have noticed the sheriff described as having the command and charge of the whole county and as representing the body of the county. The colonial sheriff inherited little of the social functions and prestige of the English official, but economic and political forces more than compensated for this loss, as well as for the loss of judicial powers, by restoring to him some of the importance his ancestor early had in England as conservator of the peace and financial officer. The office was taking on new strength in the colonies while continuing to decline in England.

The Sheriff as an Institution

A study of the origin and development of any institution is interesting but it is particularly so in the case of the sheriff. The great age of this office, its inseparability from the county, the long story of its rise and decline in England, its prevalence throughout the modern English-speaking world, and the undoubted fact that in America today, as well as in England and her colonies in the seventeenth century, the sheriff retains many of his Anglo-Saxon and Norman characteristics, make this study one of especial significance.

PART III
ILLUSTRATIVE DOCUMENTS

ILLUSTRATIVE DOCUMENTS

1. The Patent of the Sheriff's Office, England

Carolus Dei Gratia Angliae, Scotiae, Franciae, & Hiberniae, Rex, fidei defensor, &c. Omnibus ad quos praesentes literae pervenerint salutem. Sciatis quod Commissimus dilecto nobis A. B. Militi Comitat. nostrum Cantabridg. cum pertinent' custodiend. quamdiu nobis placuerit, Ita quod firmas debitas nobis reddat annuatim, ac de debitis nostris & omnibus aliis ad officium vicecomit' nostri praedict' spectant' nobis respondeat ad Scaccar' nostrum, in cujus rei Testimonium has literas nostras fieri fecimus patentes, Teste meipso apud Westm.   die   anno Regni nostri, &c.—Dalton, *Officium Vicecomitum,* cap. 2.

2. Patent of Office, Virginia, 1684

By his Excellency

Virginia ss:

Whereas by the known Laws, Customs, & Constitutions of this Colony It is provided that the Govern[or] for the time being should Nominate, Appoint & Constitute the severall high sheriffs for the Respective Counties of this his Majestyes Colony
I therefore Francis Lord Howard, Baron of Effingham, his Maties L^t & Govern[or] Genl of Virginia being well informed & assured of the Integrity & Ability of Tho Cocke Gent:, doe by these presents Nominate, Ordain, & Appoint the sd Thomas Cocke to be High-Sherriff of ye County of Henrico the next ensueing year; And doe require & Comand his ma^{ties}

Justices of ye peace holding Court on the next Court day ensueing the date hereof to administer him his Oath according to ye severall laws & Customs of this Colony; Provided that he the sd Tho Cocke do at ye sd Court held for the aforesd County enter into Bond wth Good & sufficient security for ye Well & true p forming of all & every the singular parts of ye trust & office to him by this my Comission given & granted according to the severall laws & Acts of Assembly in that Case made & provided; Given under my hand & seale the twenty fifth day of March Anno Domini one thousand six hundred eighty four, Annoque regni Caroli secundi tricesimo sexto.—Henrico County Records, 1677-92, p. 269.

3. *The Sheriff's Patent of Assistance, England*

Carolus Dei Grat' Angliae, Scotiae, Franciae, & Hiberniae, Rex, fidei defensor, &c. Archiepiscopis, Episcopis, Ducibus, Comitibus, Baronibus, Militibus, liberis Hominibus, & omnibus alijs de com. Cantabr. salutem. Cum concesserimus dilecto nobis A. B. Militi officium vicecom. nostri praed. cum pertinent,' habend. quamdiu nobis placuerit, prout in literis nostris patentibus ei inde confectis plenius continetur, vobis mandamus quod eidem A. B. tanquam vicecom. nostro cum praed' in omnibus quae ad officium illud pertinent intendentes sitis auxiliantes & respondentes. In cujus rei testimon. has literas fieri fecimus patentes, Teste meipso apud Westm.   die
    anno Regni nostri, &c.—Dalton, *Officium Vicecomitum,* cap. 2.

4. Oath of Office Taken by Sheriff William Ffarington, England, 1636

The forme of my oath at lardge—

Yee shall swear that well and trulye yee shall serve the Kinge in the office of Sheriffe of Lanc^r, and doe the Kinge pffit in all things that belongeth yo^w to doe by waye of yor office as farr forth as yo^w cann or maye. Yee shall trulye keepe the Kings rights and all that belongeth to the Crowne. Yee shall not assente to decreasse or lossing or concealm^t of the Kings rights or of his ffranchises. And where^r yee shall have knowledge that the Kings rights or the rights of his Crowne bee concealed or withdrawne, bee it in lands tenements suits ffranchises or anie other thinge, yee shall doe yor true power to make them bee restored to the Kinge again. And yf yee maye not doe itt ye shall certifie the Kinge or some of his Counsell thereof, such as yee hold for certaine will say itt unto the Kinge. Yee shall not respite the Kings debts for anie guifte or favour where yee may raise them wthout greate greevance to the debtors. Yee shall trulye and rightlye treate the people of yor Sheriffewicke and right doe as well to poore as to riche in all y^t belongeth to yor office; yee shall doe noe wrong to anie man for anie gifte of pmiss of goods, nor favour nor hate. Yee shall disturbe noe man's righte, ye shall trulye accompte before the Auditor of the Duchye of Lanc. of all them of whom yee shall anie thinge receive of the Kings debts, yee shall nothing take whereby the Kinge may lose or whereby y^t right may be disturbed letted or the Kings debts delayed, yee shall trulye return and trulye serve all the Kings Writtes as far forth as itt shalbee in yor cunninge, yee shall have none to be yor Und^r Sheriffe or anie of yor Sheriffe's Clarkes of the laste yeare passed. Yee shall take no Bailiffe into yor service but suche as yee will answer for, yee shall make eache of yor Bailiffes to make suche oathe as yo^w doe make yo^{r}self in y^t y^t belongethe to there occupacons, yee shall receive noe writt by yo^w or anie of yo^{rs} unsealed. Yee shall make yor Bailiffs of true and sufficient men in the same Countye. Yee shall doe all yor paine and diligence to destroye and make to cease all manner of Heresies and errors wthin yor Bailiwicke from tyme to tyme to all yor power, and assiste and bee helpinge to all the Ordinaries and Comissaries of the Holye Churche and favour and mainteyne them as often as yee shalbee required by the said Ordinaries and Comissaries. Yee shalbee dwellinge in yor pper pson wthin yor Bailiwicke for the tyme yee shalbee in the said office. Yee shall not lett yor Sheriffwicke or Bailiwicke thereof to farme to anie man. Yee shall trulye sett and returne reasonable and due yssues of them y^t bee wthin yor Bailiwicke after their estaits and havio^r and make yor pannels yo^{r}self. And over this in eschewinge and restraint of the manslaughters robberies and other manifold grievous offences that bee done dailye and increase in nomber and multiplye soe that the Kings true subjects may not safelye ryde nor goe to doe suche things as they have to doe, to there intollerable hurt and hindrance, yee shall truly and effectuallye with all diligence possible to yo^w execute the statutes touching the same. All wch pmises yee shall trulye and dulye doe and keepe as God helpe yo^w and by the contents of this Booke, and alsoe doe make a true and faythfull accompte of all suche pfitts and casualties as comethe and growethe of the said office, or that yee shall be chardged with in the tyme of yor occupyinge of the said office of Sheriffewicke as God yo^u helpe and by the contents of this Booke.—*Shrievalty of William Ffarington, pp. 1-3.*

5. *The Sheriff's Oath of Office, Virginia, 1641*

Yo^u shall sweare that well and truely ye shall serve the Kings Mat^ie in the office of the Sheriff of the County of Ackowmacke and doe the King's p'fitt in all things that belongeth to yo^u to doe by way of you^r Office as farr as you can or may.

You shall truely kepe the King's Rights and all that belongeth to the Crowne.

You shall truely and rightfully treate the people of yor Sheriffwick and doe right as well to the poore as to the ritch in all that belongeth to yor Office.

You shall doe noe wronge to any man for any guift or other behest or p'mise of goods for favors nor hate.

You shall disturbe noe mans rights, you shall truely retorne and truely serve all the Kings writts as farr forth as shall be to yo^u Cunning

You shall take noe Bayliffe unto yor service but such as you shall answer for

You shall make such of the Bayliffes to take such

oath as yo{u} make yo{r}selfe in that belongeth to yo{r} occupation. You shalbe dwelling in yo{r} owne p'per p'son w{th}in yo{r} Baylewick for the time that you shalbe in the same office except yo{u} are otherwise lycensed by the Governor and Counsell of this Collonye. And yo{u} shall dilligently and truely doe all other things app'taining to your sayd office of sheriffwick to the uttermost of yo{r} power. Soe help yo{u} God &C.

Md. That A. B. Gent. Chosen sheriff for the County of A. did Come before us the Commissioners appointed for the sayd County this 12{th} day of June in the 17{th} yeare of the raigne of Ou{r} Sovraigne Lord Charles in his owne p'per p'son and did acknowledge to owe to our Sovraign Lord the King Cent'm libris &C.—Accomac County Records, 1640-45, pp. 72-73.

6. *The Sheriff's Oath of Office, Maryland, 1642*

on the sixteenth day of Septemb this Oath following was administered to Edward Packer; viz: (You shall sweare that well & truely you will serve the Lord Proprietary of this Province in the office of Sheriff, & doe the Lords profit in all things that belongeth to you to doe by way of your office as far forth as you may; you shall truely & rightfully treat the people of your sherifwick, & doe right as well to poore as to rich, in all that belongeth to your office; ye shall truely returne and truely serve all writts & warrants lawfully directed to you, to your cunning; and in all other things ye shall well & faithfully discharge the office of Sheriff committed unto

you, to your skill & power. So helpe you God.)—
*Maryland Archives: Proceedings of the Council,
1636-67*, p. 117.

7. Jailer's Bond to Sheriff, England, 1636

A Bond in £ 1000 from Thomas Covell of Lancaster Esq. and John Rigmaiden of Lancaster Yœman to W^m. ffarington of Worden Esq. Dat. 12 April 1636.

The condition—That ffarington as High Sheriff has appointed Covell to be the Keeper of all such prisoners as shall be arrested or attached by any writ warrant or Precept made in the name of the said High Sheriff or of his Under Sheriff or any Justice of the Peace within the s^d Co. and committed to His Majestys Prison att the Castle of Lancaster and the same safely to keep from escape &c and also to exonerate and save harmless the s^d. High Sheriff from all manner of Judgments executions fynes chardges troubles an incumbrances which shall or may hereafter grow or happen to be taxed imposed estreated or levied upon the s^d Sheriff as Sheriff of the Co. af^d. by reason of any such escape or escapes or any other matter whatso^r. touching the keeping of the said Gaole if s^d. Tho. Covell or his deputy shall unlawfully discharge or sett at liberty any such Prisoner delivered to his Custody without the speciale Warrant under the seal of the s^d. High Sheriff, or shall not attend the s^d. High Sheriff when required by his office that then this obligation &c or else &c.

Tho. Covell
John Rigmaiden

—Raines MSS, XXIII, 87.

8. Writ of Election, England, 1603

The writ for the Choice of the Knights, Citizens, and Burgesses, directed to the Sheriff of every County:

Jacobus, Dei Gratia, &c. Vicecomiti Buck. Salutem. Quia de Avisamento et Assensu Concilii nostri, pro quibusdam arduis et urgentibus Negotiis, Nos, Statum, et defensionem Regni nostri Angliae, et Ecclesiae Anglicaniae, concernentibus, quoddam Parliamentum nostrum, apud Civitatem nostram Westmonasterii, Decimo nono Die Martii proxime futuro, teneri ordinavimus, et ibidem, cum Praelatis, Magnatibus, et Proceribus dicti Regni nostri Colloquium habere et Tractatum; tibi praecipimus, firmiter injungentes, quod, facta Proclamatione in proximo Comitatu tuo post Receptionem huius Brevis nostri tenendo, de Die et Loco praedictis duos Milites, Gladiis cinctos, magis idoneos, et discretos, Comitatus praedicti, et de qualibet Civitate Comitatus illius duos Cives, et de quolibet Burgo duos Burgenses, de discretioribus et magis sufficientibus, libere et indifferenter per illos, qui Proclamationi huiusmodi interfuerunt, juxta Formam Statutorum inde editorum et provisorum, eligi, et Nomina eorundem Militum, Civium, et Burgensium, sic eligendorum, in quibusdam Indenturis, inter te et illos, qui hujusmodi Electioni interfuerint, inde conficiendis, licet hujusmodi Eligendi praesentes fuerint vel absentes, inseri, eosque ad dictos Diem et Locum venire facias; ita quod iidem Milites plenam et sufficientem Potestatem pro se et Communitate Comitatus illius, ac dicti

Cives et Burgenses pro se et Communitate Civitatum et Burgorum praedictorum, divisim ab ipsos habeant, ad faciendum, et consentiendum hiis, quae tunc ibidem et Communi Consilio dicti Regni nostri (favente Domino) contigerint ordinari super Negotiis antedictis; ita quod, pro defectu Potestatis hujusmodi, seu propter improvidam Electionem Militum, Civium, aut Burgensium praedictorum, dicta Negotia infecta non remaneant. Nolumus autem, quod tu, nec aliquis alius Vicecomes dicti Regni nostri, aliqualiter sit electus. Et Electionem illam, in pleno Comitatu tuo factam, distincte et aperte, sub Sigillo tuo, et Sigilis eorum, qui Electioni illi interfuerint, nobis in Cancellariam nostram ad dictos Diem et Locum certifices indilati remittens inde alteram Partem Indenturarum praedictarum, praesentibus consutam, una cum hoc Brevi, Teste Meipso, apud Westmonasterium, Tricesimo primo Die Januarii, Anno Regni nostri, Angliae, Franciae, et Hiberniae, Primo, et Scotiae Tricesimo septimo.

Form of Return of the Writ into the Crown Office in the Chancery:

Haec Indentura, facta Sexto Die Martii, Anno, &c. inter Majorem, Ballivos, et Burgenses, Burgi de C. &c. in Comitatu D. ex una Parte, et E. P. Armigerum, Vicecomitem Comitatus praedicti, —— virtute Praecepti nobis in ea Parte directi, ex unanimi Consensu pariter et Assensu nostro, eligimus W. D. et C. P. Armigeros, Burgenses Burgi praedicti, ad interessendum pro nobis ad Parliamentum dicti Domini Regis, apud Civitatem Westmonasterii Decimo nono Die instantis Mensis Martii tenendum; dantes, et per praesentes consedentes, praefatis Burgensibus, conjunctim et divisim, pro nobis, et Successoribus nostris, plenam et sufficientem Potestatem, ad faciendum et consentiendum hiis, quae ad Communi Concilio dicti Regni dicto Domino Regi (favente Deo) contigerint ordinari. In cujus Rei Testimonium, uni Parti harum Indenturarum, penes nos praefatos Majorem, Ballivos, et Burgenses remanenti, praefatus Vicecomes Sigillum suum apposuit, alteri vero Parti dicti Major, Ballivi, et Burgenses Sigillum suum commune apposuerunt. Dat. apud C. praedict. Die et Anno supradictis.—*Journals of the House of Commons, 1547-1628,* p. 140.

9. Writ of Election, Maryland, 1670

These are to Authorise and require you to call together this pres^t month of december four or more of the Commissioners of your County with the Clerk whom you are hereby required to impower to sit as a Court and during their sitting by Virtue of your Office to make or Cause to be made publick Proclamation thereby giving notice to all the freemen of your said County who are within the said County Visible seated Plantations of fifty Acres of Land at the least or Visible personal Estates to the Value of forty Pounds Sterling at the least requiring them to appear at the next County Court to be holden for the said County at a Certain day in the month next following after such Proclamation made for the election and Choosing of Deputies and Delegates to serve for your said County in a General Assembly shortly after to be called by special writ at which time and place according to the said Proclamation the said freemen so required to appear or the Major Part of such of them as shall thereupon appear shall and may and are hereby Authorized and required to elect and choose four several sufficient freemen of your said County each of them having a visible seated Plantation of fifty Acres of Land at the least or a Visible personal Estate of Forty Pounds Sterling at the least within your said County and you shall Give Authority to each of them severally and Respectively by four several and respective Indentures under their hands and seals to be deputy and Delegate for your said County and to appear and serve as Deputy and Delegate for your said County at the next General Assembly in case he shall be thereunto summoned by a particular writt for that Purpose to be directed to him from the Lieutenant General of this Province for the time being and to do and Consent to those things which then by the favour of God shall there happen to be Ordained by the Lord and Proprietary or his said Lieutenant with the advice and Consent of the Great Council of the said Province concerning such Occasions and Affairs as shall Relate to the Government State and defence of the said Province which said Indentures shall be between you the Sheriff on the one part and the said freemen electing on the other part and shall bear date the same day upon which the said Election shall be made and shall mention the time and place of such election and the Person so Elected and Shall be signed and Sealed each part of them as well by the said Sheriff as by the said freemen by whom the said Election shall be made and that upon such election you the said Sheriff shall so soon as Conveniently may be certify and transmit to the Chancellor of this said Province for the time being one part of the said several and respective Indentures close sealed up under Your hand and seal and directed to the Lieutenant General of this said Province and also to the said Chancellor and the other part of the said Indentures you the said Sheriff are to keep for your Iustification. Given under my hand and Seal this 18th day of December in the 39th Year of the dominion of Cecilius &c Annoq Domini 1670.—*Maryland Archives: Proceedings of the Council, 1667-87/8,* pp. 77-78.

10. The Sheriff to Collect Salary of Parochial Burgess, Virginia

Nov. 19, 1663.

At a Vestrey held for the p'ish
of Lancaster at ye house of
Mr Henry Corbin &c.

It is further Ordered that there be leveyed upon ye prish for the defraying of M^r. Henry Corbins Charge in two assemblies sume of ffoure thousand seven hundred ffourty and three pounds of Tobacco, and that ye Sherriff is desired to Collect Same, and Mr Cuthbert Potter is hereby appointed to pr fect the List for this p^rish.

Cuthbert Potter
Abra: Weekes
Thomas Willis
Robert Chowning
} John Vause
Henry Corbin
Richard Perrott
} Vestreymen.

—Christ Church, Middlesex, Vestry Book, p. 2.

11. *The Sheriff to Supervise Election of the Vestry, Virginia*

June 10, 1708.

At a Court held at the Capitol, the 10th of June, 1708, Present—The Hon^bl the President and Council.

Whereas, the sheriff of the County of York is directed to attend the Election of the Vestry of Charles parish on Tuesday the 29th of this present month, and to take the poll at the same for his better guidance and directions therein, & for avoiding all tumult and confusion, which usually happens on such occasions, It is ordered that every freeholder and Householder paying Seatt and Lett in the parish, and no other have vote at the said Election, and for clearing any doubts that may happen as to any persons being a freeholder, or householder, the Sheriff is impowered to administer to such persons an oath—required in the same manner as is directed by Law in the Election of Burgesses; the said Sheriff shall separately demand, and accordingly take in writing from every person having vote in the said Election, the names of twelve men whom such person thinks most fitt to be vestrymen in the said parish, and haveing so set down in writing each particular Election list or number of twelve men, he shall then examine all the said Lists and shall declare those twelve men to be the Vestry whom (upon scrutiny) he shall find to have most votes; And ordered that the said Sheriff make Return of his proceedings, together with the severall lists aforesaid to the Council office.

This order to be kept private 'till ye election

     Wil. Robertson, Clk. Cort.
     Lau^r Smith, Sherf, Y. C.

—*Virginia Calendar of State Papers,* I, 122.

12. Warrant for Summoning the Posse Comitatus, England, 1643

Wigorn. S. S. Willm Russell, Baronet, High Sheriff of the said County, to Francis Smith, gent., one of the High Constables of the Hundred of Halfshire.

Whereas there is information given that there have of late many unlawful and rebellious forces and riotous assemblies been made and are like to continue or rather increase in some parts of the County tending much to the disturbance of the peace thereof, and to the spoiling of his Majesty's good subjects and their estates therein and that certain of the justices of the peace and others his Majesty's Commissioners for preserving the peace of this County taking it into their serious consideration have thought fit to raise the power of the County according to law for suppressing such assemblies, and have directed me as Sheriff to issue forth warrants to that purpose. These are therefore to will and require you, and in his Majesty's name straitly to charge and command you by the Assistance of the Petty Constables within your division to summon and bring in upon Tuesday next being the second of May next to the great Meadow called Pitchcroft near the City of Worcester all persons Whatsoever within your division above the age of sixteen years and under the age of three score years and able to travel, with such arms or weapons as they have or can provide to join with me and the rest of the justices and Commissioners for securing of this County for suppressing of such notorious Assemblies and Rebellious Forces, whereof they may not fail upon pain of imprisonment, fine and ransome according to the statute in that case provided, And hereof fail not upon peril of the strictest punishment the law can inflict. Dated at Worcester, this 29th day of April 1643

         Will. Russell

To the Constable of Elmley Lovet
I charge you in his Majesty's name to execute your office according to the Warrant above written.
         Francis Smith
—*Diary of Henry Townshend of Elmley Lovett, 1640-1663*, II, 121-22.

13. *Warrant from the Justices of the Peace to the Sheriff to Summon the Sessions, England, 1624*

To the Sheriffe of the Countie of Northampton
Accordinge to his Maties Commission under the great

Seale of England to us and others his Maties Justices of the peace of the County of Northampton directed. We will and require you in his Ma^{tes} name to make out summons of the Sessions of the peace in usuall Course to be holden at the Castle of Northampton for the said County of Northampton on Tuesdaie the XXVth day of this instant moneth of May. And yt yow retorne a sufficient Jurie to serue for the body of your said County. And to giue due warninge to the Jurors to make theire appearance at the said tyme and place for the better execution of his Ma^{tes} service. And that yow likewise proceede in the retorne and summons of such hundred Juries of the said County as by Course are them to serue, hereof faile yow not at your perill. Dated the 10th day of May in the 22th yeare of his Ma^{tes} Reigne of England, and of Scotland ye L V i jth

      H. Oxenford: Exeter Robert: Spencer
(Autograph)
      William Spencer fr. Harvey Erasmus Drydon
(Signatures)
      Edward Onley Richard Knightley.

Endorsement

By virtue of this warrant to me directed I haue summoned the Sessions of the peace for the County of Northampton in usuall course to be holden at the day and place within written, And I have also summoned X X i i i j^{er} good and lawful menne of the said County to appeare at the said day and place within written to enquire for our soueraigne lord the kinge and the body of the County aforesaid, And I haue alsoe summoned those X X i i i j^{er} good and lawfull men of every Hundred of the Hundreds of Corby: Higham fferrers: Polebrooke: Warden & Willobrooke (being the hundreds which by due course are to serve at this Sessions) to be and appeare before his Ma^{tes} Justices of the peace of the County aforesaid at the Sessions to doe and performe such service as on his Ma^{tes} behalfe they shalbe then and there enioyned, as by this warrant I ame commaunded.

The Residue of the execucion of this warrant is contayned in certayne Scedules and Pannells herunto annexed.

Edwardus Shugborowe Ar' vic'

—Joan Wake, *Quarter Sessions Records of the County of Northampton*, I, App. p. 259.

14. Commission of the Peace, England

George II. by the grace of God etc. to A, B, C, D etc. greeting.

Know that we have assigned you, jointly and severally, and every one of you, our justices to keep our peace in our county of W. And to keep and to cause to be kept all ordinances and statutes for the good of the peace, and for preservation of the same, and for the quiet rule and government of our people made, in all and singular their articles in our said county (as well within liberties as without) according to the force, form, and effect of the same; and to chastise and punish all persons that offend against the form of those ordinances or statutes, or any one of them, in the aforesaid county, as it ought to be done according to the form of those ordinances and statutes; And to cause to come before you, or any of you, all those who to any one or more of our people concerning their bodies or the firing of their houses have used threats, to find sufficient security for the peace, or their good behaviour, towards us and our people; and if they shall refuse to find such security, then them in our prisons until they shall find such security to cause to be safely kept.

We have also assigned you, and every two or more of you (of whom any one of you *(quorum)* the aforesaid A, B, C, D etc. we will shall be one) our justices to enquire the truth more fully, by the oath of good and lawful men of the aforesaid county, by whom the truth of the matter shall be the better known, of all and all manner of felonies, poisonings, inchantments, soceries, art magick, trespasses, forestallings, regratings, ingrossings, and extortions whatsoever; and of all and singular other crimes and offences, of which the justices of our peace may or ought lawfully to enquire, by whomsoever and after what manner soever in the said county done or perpetrated, or which shall happen to be there done or attempted; And also of all those who in the aforesaid county in companies against our peace, in disturbance of our people, with armed force have gone or rode, or hereafter shall presume to go or ride; And also of all those who have there lain in wait, or hereafter shall presume to lay in wait, to maim or cut or kill our people; And also of all victuallers, and all and singular other persons, who in the abuse of weights or measures, or in selling victuals, against the form of the ordinances and statutes, or any one of them therefore made for the common benefit of England and our people thereof, have offended or attempted, or hereafter shall presume in the said county to offend or attempt; And also of all sheriffs, bailiffs, stewards, constables, keepers of gaols, and other officers, who in the execution of their offices about the premises, or any of them, have unduly behaved themselves, or hereafter shall presume to behave themselves unduly, or have been, or shall happen hereafter to be careless, remiss, or negligent in our aforesaid county; And of all and singular articles, and circumstances, and all other things whatsoever, that concern the premises of any of them, by whomsoever, and after what manner soever, in our aforesaid county done or perpetrated, or which hereafter shall there happen to be done or attempted in what manner soever; And to inspect all indictments whatsoever so before you or any of you taken or to be taken, or before others late our justices of the peace in the aforesaid county made or taken, and not yet determined; and to make and continue processes thereupon, against all and singular the persons so indicted, or who before you hereafter shall happen to be indicted; until they can be taken, surrender themselves, or be outlawed; And to hear and determine all and singular the felonies, poisonings, inchantments, soceries, arts magick, trespasses, forestallings, regratings, ingrossings, extortions, unlawful assemblies, indictments aforesaid, and all and singular other the premises, according to the laws and statutes of England, as in the like case it hath been accustomed, or ought to be done; And the same offenders, and every of them for their offences by fines, ransoms, amerciaments, forfeitures, and other means as according to the law and custom of England or form of the ordinances and statutes aforesaid, it has been accustomed, or ought to be done to chastise and punish.

Provided always, that if a case of difficulty, upon the determination of any the premisses, before you, or any two or more of you, shall happen to arise; then let judgment in no wise be given thereon, before you, or any two or more of you, unless in the presence of one of our justices of the one or other bench, or of one of our justices appointed to hold the assizes in the aforesaid county.

And therefore we command you and every of you, that to keeping the peace, ordinances, statutes, and all and singular other the premises, you diligently apply yourselves; and that at certain days and places, which you, or any such two or more of you as is aforesaid shall appoint for these purposes, into the premisses ye make inquiries; and all and singular the premisses hear and determine, and perform and fulfil them in the aforesaid form, doing therein what to justice appertains, according to the law and custom of England: Saving to us the amercements, and other things to us therefrom belonging.

And we command by the tenor of these presents our sheriff of W. that at certain days and places, which you, or any such two or more of you, as is aforesaid, shall make known to him, he cause to come before you, or such two or more of you as aforesaid, so many and such good and lawful men of his bailiwick (as well within liberties as without) by whom the truth of the matter in the premises shall be the better known and inquired into

Lastly, we have assigned you the aforesaid A. B. keeper of the rolls of our peace in our said county. And therefore you shall cause to be brought before you and your said fellows, at the days and places aforesaid, the writs, precepts, processes, and indictments aforesaid, that they may be inspected, and by a due course determined as is aforesaid.

In witness whereof we have caused these our letters to be made patent. Witness ourself at Westminster etc.—Copied from W. S. Holdsworth's *History of English Law,* 2nd ed., I, 443-44. (The commission of the peace of 1590 remained unchanged until the nineteenth century. This is a translation from the Latin).

15. *Commission of the Peace, Maryland, 1681*

Charles Absolute Lord and Prop[ry] of the Province of Maryland & Avalon Lord Baron of Baltemore &c To Cap[t] Samuel Bourne, Roger Brooke, Richard Ladd, John Griggs, Thomas Sterling, Thomas Brooke, Richard Marsham, George Lingan, John Craycroft, ffrancis Collier, ffrancis Hutchins, and

Samuel Taylor gentl greeteing. Know yee that wee for the greate trust and confidence wee have in your ffidelityes circumspections, prudences and wisdomes, have Constituted, ordeined and appointed, and doe by these presents constitute ordeine and appoint you the said Samuel Bourne, Roger Brooke, Richard Ladd, and John Griggs, Thomas Sterling, Thomas Brooke, Richard Marsham, George Lingan, John Craycroft ffrancis Collier ffrancis Hutchins and Samuel Taylor gentl Comissioners jointly & severally to keepe the peace in Calvert County, and to keepe and cause to be kept all Laws and orders made for the good and conservation of the peace, and for the quiett rule & government of the people in all and every the Articles of the same, and to chastise and punish all persons Offending against the forme of any the Lawes and orders of our s^d Province or of any of them in Calvert County aforesaid as according to the forme of those lawes and orders shall be fitt to be done, We have also constituted and ordeined you and every four or more of you (of which you the said Samuel Bourne, Roger Brooke, Richard Ladd, and John Griggs (unless some one of our Councill be present) are also to be) Our Commissioners to enquire by the oathes of good and lawfull men of your County aforesaid of all manner of ffellonies, Witchcrafts, Inchantm^{ts}, Sorcerys, Magic, arts, Trespasses, fforestallings, Ingrosseings and extortions whatsoever and of all and singular other misdeeds and Offences of which Justices of the peace in

England may or ought lawfully to enquire by whomsoever or whensoever done or perpetrated or which hereafter shall happen to be done or perpetrated in the County aforesaid against the Laws and orders of our said Province, Provided you proceed not in any of the Cases aforesaid to take life or member, but that in every such case you send the prisoners with their Indictments and the whole matter depending before you to the next Provinciall Court to be holden for our said Province, whensoever or wheresoever to be holden, there to be tryed. And further wee doe hereby Authorise you to issue Writts, processes, Arrests, and Attachm^{ts} To hold plea of Oyer and terminer, and after judgment Execution to award in all causes civill whether in actions reall or personall according to the Lawes orders and reasonable customs made and used in our said Province of Maryl^d in which causes civill soe to be tryed Wee Doe constitute ordeine and appoint you Samuel Bourne, Roger Brooke, Richard Ladd and John Griggs to be Judges as aforesaid, unless some One of our Councill be then in Court And therefore we command you that you diligently intend the keepeing of the peace Laws and orders, and all and singular other the premisses, and at certain dayes appointed according to Act of Assembly in that case provided and such places which you or any four or more of you as aforesaid shall in that behalf appoint Yee make Enquiries upon the premisses and perform and fullfill the same in forme aforesaid, doeing therein that which to Justice appertaineth according to the Laws orders and reasonable Customs of our said Province, Saveing to us the Amerciam^{ts} and other things thereof to us belonging And therefore wee command the Sheriff of the said County of Calvert by vertue of these presents that at the Dayes and places aforesaid which you or any such four or more of you as aforesaid shall make knowne to him to give his attendance on you, and if need require to cause to come before you or any such four or more or you as aforesaid such and soe many good and lawfull men of your County by whom the truth in the premisses may the better be knowne and enquired of, And further you shall cause to be brought before you at the said Dayes and places, the writts precepts processes, and Indictm^{ts} to your Court and Jurisdiction belonging, that the same may be inspected and by a due course Determined as aforesaid. Given at our City of St Maries under the greate Seale of our said Province of Maryland the Eight and twentieth Day of July in the Sixth yeare of our Dominion &c. Annoq Dmi One thousand Six hundred Eighty and One.—*Maryland Archives: Proceedings of the Council, 1671-81,* pp. 396-98.

16. Description of a Procession to the Assizes, England

On Sunday last, Sir Richard Arkwright, Knight, sheriff of the County (of Derby), arrived at Derby, accompanied by a great number of Gentlemen, &c on horseback; his javelin men (thirty in number, exclusive of bailiffs, &c. &c.) dressed in the richest liveries ever seen there on such an occasion. Their coats were dark blue elegantly trimmed with gold lace; scarlet waistcoats laced with gold, and buff coloured velvet Breeches; they had also blue great Coats, buckled behind after the manner of his Majesty's Regiment of Horse Guards; their Hats were smartly cocked, with gold button, Cap and tassels; they all rode on Black Horses, and had new bridles given them by the sheriff, also new boots, &c. The Trumpeters were mounted on Gray Horses, and elegantly dressed in Scarlet and gold. The High Sheriff's coach was very elegant and fashionable, with plated Furniture, lined with drab cloth, and bound with Livery-lace; purple Festoons at the Windows, trimmed with silver fringe; the Body painted Batwing colour, with a white Border; the Arms painted in Mantle; carriage and wheels painted red and pic'd in the same colour as the Body; the Coach-box ornamented with an elegant Hammer-cloth, and very elegant plated Harness. We must not forget to inform our Readers that Sir Richard during the whole of the Assize provided a plentiful Table, with the choicest Wines, &c. for such Gentlemen as pleased to partake of the noble Banquet.—*Manchester Mercury,* March 27, 1787. (I am indebted to Professor Witt Bowden of the University of Pennsylvania for this fine picture.)

17. *The Sheriff's Writ of Discharge, England*

Carolus, &c. dilecto sibi R. S. Armigero nuper vicecom. Cantabr. salutem. Cum concesserimus dilecto, &c. nobis A. B. militi Com. nostrum praed' custodiend. quamdiu nobis placuerit, prout in literis nostris patentibus ei inde concess. plenius continetur, tibi praecipimus quod eidem A. B. com. nostr. praed. cum pertinentiis, una cum rotulis, brevibus, memorand. & omnibus aliis ad officium vicecom. praed' spectant' quae in custodia tua existunt, per indenturas inde inter te, & praefatum A. B. debiti conficiend. liberes. Teste meipso apud Westmonaster quinto die, &c.—Dalton, *Officium Vicecomitum*, cap. 2.

18. Rotation of Office, Virginia, 1668-69

Gentlemen—I understand that Capt Hay your late sheriffe is deced & have therefore appointed a very honest Gentleman Major Robert Baldry to whom it alsoe belongs by his place in your Commission sherriffe of Yorke County for the ensuing yeare, who is accordingly to be admitted & sworn at yor next Court Jan'y the 23th 1668

Yo^r friend & servt
William Berkeley

—York County Records, 1664-72, p. 224.

19. Military Command Given to the Sheriff, Maryland, 1648

By the Governo^r of Mary-Land.

Relying uppon yor faythfullness & courage I doe hereby committ unto yo^w & adde unto yor office of High-Sheriffe of the County of Kent, the Command of all the Militia of the s^d County, requyring yo^w to take charge thereof: And uppon any inuasion from abroad or mutiny, insolence, or other breatch of Peace att home or indaungering the publik safety of yor County, to encounter & suppresse the same, in the best & speediest manner yo^w may: And to rayse & leuy the force of the s^d County to th^t purpose, or any part thereof, as there shall be cause. And I doe hereby requyre all p^{r}sons able to beare Armes wthin the s^d County, to be obedient unto yo^w uppon such paynes & perills, as the offence agst Military discipline shall deserue by the Law of Armes or censure of the Prouinciall Cou^{rt}. Gyuen att S^{t}maries this iith 9^{ber} 1648

Tho: Greene

To Mr Henry Morgan
Sheriffe of Kent County
—*Maryland Archives: Proceedings of the Council, 1636-67,* p. 197.

20. *The Coroner to Summon the Sheriff, Maryland, 1684*

Maryland SS.

Ordered that the Coroner of Cecill County forthwith upon sight hereof summons William Peirce genll high Sheriff of the said County & William Nowell, now or late his Deputy, that all excuses set apart they be and personally appear before his Lordship's Council at the City of St Maries the first day of the next Provincial Court there to be holden to answer unto such things as shall and there be objected against them. Whereof let there be noe faile, and for soe doeing this shall be a sufficient warrant. Given at City of St Maries 2 Dec. 1684

 To the Coroner   Signed p ord^r
 of Cecil County.   J LL. Cl Consil

—*Maryland Archives: Proceedings of the Council, 1681-85/6*, p. 326.

21. The Sheriff's Warrant to Take the Lists of Tithables, Maryland, 1666

Theis are to will & require you yt by ye tenth daye of octob^r next you Cause a list to be taken of all ye tithables within yor County & in ye said list ye name & surname of each tithable person & the house of his abode be distinctly sett downe & a Copy thereof fayre written & sent imediately up to ye Governor & Councell and another Copy of ye said list sett up att yor Court house att yor next County Court to remayne there for ye whole yeare to ye end y^t iff any error be therein they may be Corrected & ye same Certified to ye Governor & Councell before ye next provinciall Court being to be held on ye 16th day of october next ensueing herein fayle not as you will answer ye Contrary and for soe doeing this shall be yor warrant Given under my hand & seale this 22th day of August A° 1666.

             Charles Calvert

To Stephen Horsey gent
highe sherriffe of Somersett County
—*Somerset County Records, Liber Bl, 1665-68*, p. 24.

22. *A Typical Writ with the Sheriff's Return*

Charles & To the sherriffe of Talbott County greeting whereas att a Court held for Talbott County the 17th day of 9^{ber} 1685 in a Certaine Cause depending before our justices att our County Court afsd between Cha: Robinson plt and Tho: Brown dft in a plea of debt, the said plt recovered judgmt ag^t. the deft for eight hundreds p^{ds} of tobb wth Costs of suit, and forasmuch as execution hath not thereupon as yett issued we therefore Comand you that by good and lawfull men of your balywick you make known unto the said Tho: Brown that he be and appeare before our justices att our next Court to be held for Talbott County the third Tuesday of X^{ber} next to shew Cause if any he have why execution shall not issue ag^t. him for the judgmt af^d and how you shall execut. this wr^{tt}. that you make known to our said justices wth. the persons names by whom you soe make known the same, and have you there this wr^{tt}. And for soe doeing this shall be y^r. warr^{tt}. wittness Ed^{wd} man Gent. Chife Justice of our said Court and seale of Talbott County this 17th. day of 9^{ber} in the 12th. year of our Dom^{on} & Ann^o Domo 1687

Nic^o: Lowe C^{lk}

Endorsed on back of writ

By vertue of this wr^{tt}. to the justices wthin wr^{tt}en I Certifie y^t I have made knowne unto ye wthin written Tho. Browne soe y^t he be and app^a. before ye justices wthin written att ye time & place wthin Contained to show Cause if any he have by

Nath^a. Teagle & Jno. Man good and lawfull men as this writt exacteth & requireth

     Nich^o. Gouldsbourough sub sherr
—Talbot County Records, Liber N N, 1686-89—no pagination.

23. *The Sheriff and Coroners to Recover the Crown's Casual Revenues, Virginia, 1700*

Whereas severall Buoys, Cables, Anchors and other things belonging to his Maj^{ties} Ships Merch^t Ships and other vessells are often times Clandestinely taken up and carryed away by severall Covetious and Evil Disposed Persons soe that his Maj^{tie} or the Right own^{rs} thereto are hereby defrauded of their Just Right to the same and whereas Especiall at this time severall goods and merchandizes may be found floating upon the water in the Bay of Chisapeake or upon some other haven River or Creek in this his Maj^{ties} Colony and Dominion or may be drove on shore and there privately taken up and carryed away Therefore I Francis Nicholson Esqr his Maj^{ties} Lieut. and Govern^r Generall of Virg^a by and with the advice and consent of his Maj^{ties} Honble Councill of State doe hereby Command and require all his Maj^{ties} Coron^{rs} and Sheriffs in their respective Counties and Stations to use their utmost Endeavour to take and secure all Wrecks, Buoys, Cables, Anchors, Boates or other goods and merchandizes which they shall find in or floating upon the water or Drove upon the Shore and all such goods and things as may be accounted for

Floatsam Jetsam or Lagan and all Waifs Strays and Fellon's goods, and Give me an acc't thereof from time to time and I doe likewise charge and Command all other his Maj^ties good and Loving Subjects that they doe not presume to Conceale or Convert to their owne use all or any the aforementioned particulars that by them hath been or shall be hereafter taken up but that they Immediately repair to some one of his Maj^ties Coron^rs or to the Sheriff of the County where such thing or things were taken who is to give me an account thereof upon which I will take care that such Person or Persons shall have allowance for Salvage for what they shall take up and safely secure Given under my hand and his Maj^ties Seale of the Colony, this 23^d day of May 1700 in the Twelfth yeare of his Maj^ties Reign

Fr Nicholson

—*Executive Journals of the Council of Colonial Virginia*, II, 86-87.

24. Deodand

Court for Upper Northampton, 17 July, 1672.

Whereas it appeared to the Court by verdict of Coroners jury of inquest that a mare formerly belonging to Pierce Davis & after a "Deidand" to his Maties for the untimely death of Nath^ll Starky occasioned through a fall from sd mare and whereas it likewise appeered that by order of sd Pierce Davis sd mare was removed & carried away from place where fact was committed, now upon petition of Mr Jno Culpeper on behalf of his Majesty it is judged by the Court & ordered that sd Pierce Davis forthwith deliver unto the sd Mr. Culpeper High Sheriff on behalf of his Majesty sd mare to be forfeited to his Majesty & pay all costs of suit *als exec*—Accomac County Records, 1671-73, p. 116.

25. Commission of the Commander, Virginia, 1626

To all whome &c. Knowe y^t I Sir George Yeardly wth ye advise and consent of ye Counsell of estate here resident, doe by these presents give leave and lycence unto Captain Nethann^{ell} Basse and his associatts, to repossesse & —— his land at Warrasquoake Called Bass s banke, and doe hereby Charge and Comaund him presently to ffortifie his and ther houses, wthin one very defencible pallizade, and to keepe due watch now and ward at all tymes, as hee will answere ye Contrary to his perrill, And I doe by these p ntes give power and Authority unto him ye said Capt. Basse to Comaund and governe all ye people, now Resident, or wch shall or may come to reside at ye said Basses banke, according to his best discrecon in all Causes y^t shall appertaine to his place and calling as Com (mander) of ye said plantacon, and I doe hereby Charge & Comaund all ye said people in all things, and uppon all occasions, appertayning to —— as Comaunder That they give all due respect and willingly obey and execute ye directions and —— of him, and be ayding and assisting (?) unto him ye said Capt Basse, as they will answere ye Contrary to the —— and for ye greater ease and benefitt of ye said plantacon, I doe by these presents give suitable power and Authority unto ye said Capt: Basse & other of ye most honnest understanding and sufficient men, hee can make choyse of in ye said plantacon, or any two of them, and ye said Capt Bass being one, to here and determyne as smale varyances arising betweene party and party, not exceeding a hundred pound waight of tobacco and to punish all such, as are under his Comaund y^t shall offend in drunkennes & swearing, —— and necklect in frequenting of devine service, or ye like according to ye laws of England, in y^t case provided and proclamacons here published concearneing ye same, and if any —— shalbe a notorious and incorigible offender in any of ye afore said synnes, —— us or shall not Receave ye holy Comonyne, thrise at ye least in ye yeare, to deliver ye names to ye Gov(er)ner and Counsell of Estate, at ye quarter sessions, And I doe hereby give full power, and Authority to Nominate and a pointe sufficient officer, to bee a provice Marshall for ye said plantacon And hee to keepe a register of all such as shall any way delinquent, and of such as shall dye from tyme to tyme, and also of all —— and fynes whatsoever And if any of ye said plantacon shall decease, either making will or intestate shall praise ye goods and chattles of ye deceased, & present in Court, to ye Governer and Counsell a true and iust Inventory therof wthin xx days next after ye said parties decease, And if any of ye said plantacon shall Comitt a Cappitall offence, as Treason, Murther, or ffellony y^t then the said provice Marshall, by warrant from ye said Captaine Basse, in his absence from any two of his assistance shall apprehend and atach ye body of such offender, and him or them

to take into his Custowdy and saffe keeping, and to bring him or them to ye Governor and Counsell to James Citty, to be tryd according to ye Law
In witness
  By the Governer
  & Captaine generall
    of Verginia

—Randolph MSS, 1626-34. Document split by copyist on sheets 12 and 13. Note the close similarity of this commission to those issued to the commanders of the Isle and County of Kent, *Maryland Archives: Proceedings of the Council, 1636-67,* pp. 124-25, 182-83.

26. *Oath of the County Clerk, Virginia, 1673-74*

You shall sweare that with the best of yor desterity & skill you shall use, exercise and execute the Clerkes place & office of this County Court, during the tyme you shall continue & remaine therein, neither shall or will take or receive by any device Color, or meanes whatsoever any ffee or reward of any person or persons whatsoever for the altering of any Record nor consent to the same, neither shall you deferre any person or persons for expedicon money but shall faithfully to the best of yor understanding & knowledge draw upp all orders of this Court & finally doe all other matters & things incident & apperteyneing to the said place of Clerke for the tyme you shall contine therein

So helpe you God
—Middlesex County Records, 1673-80, p. 6[2]

27. Oath of The Constable, Virginia, 1640-45

You shall sweare that you shall well and truly serve Our Sovraigne Lord the King in the Office of a Constable. You shall see and cause his Maties peace to be well and dewly kept and p'formed according to your power w^{th}in you^r lymitt. You shall arrest all such p'sons as in yor sight and p'sence shall committ or make any affray, ryott, or other breach of his Maties peace You shall doe yor best indeavor upon complaynt to you made to app^rhend all ffelons, barrettours, revolturs or p'sons ryotously assembled, and yf any such offender shall make resistance wth fforce, you shall levye huy and cry, and shall p'sue them to the utmost of yor lymitt and give warning to the next Constable for his or their ffurther p'suing. You shall have a watchfull eye to such p'sons as shall keepe any victualling and drinking houses, to all such as shall unlawfully frequent such places. You shall well and dewly execute all Acts of Assembly to wch the sayd Acts command you, as also all p'cepts and warrants to you directed from the Governor or any of the Counsell, or any of the Commissioners for the Monthely Courts where to yor lymitt belongs And you shall well and duely according to yor knowledge power and ability, doe and execute all other things belonging to the office of a Constable, soe long as you shall continue in this office, soe help you God ec.—Accomac County Records, 1640-45, p. 82.

BIBLIOGRAPHY

I. ENGLAND

A. NON-CONTEMPORANEOUS ACCOUNTS, BIBLIOGRAPHIES, AND GUIDES

Cheyney, E. P., *A History of England from the Defeat of the Armada to the Death of Elizabeth with an Account of English Institutions During the Later Sixteenth and Early Seventeenth Centuries.* 2 vols. New York, 1914, 1926. Part VIII, a description of local government, is authoritative and stimulating. Professor Cheyney has opened up a fertile and important field of research that had hardly been touched.

Gardiner, S. R., *History of England from 1603 to 1642.* 10 vols. London, 1883-84.

―――― *History of the Great Civil War, 1642-49.* 4 vols. London, 1886-91.

―――― *History of the Commonwealth and Protectorate.* 3 vols. London, 1894-1903.

Giuseppi, M. S., *A Guide to the Manuscripts Preserved in the Public Record Office.* 2 vols. London, 1923-24.

Holdsworth, W. S., *History of English Law.* Vol. I, Appendix. Boston, 1908.

Hulme, Harold, "The Sheriff as a Member of the House of Commons from Elizabeth to Cromwell," *Journal of Modern History*, Vol. I (September, 1929).

Humphreys, A. L., *Handbook to County Bibliography, Being a Bibliography of Bibliographies Relating to the Counties and Towns of Great Britain and Ireland.* London, 1917.

Jacob's *Law Dictionary.* 1729.

Johnson, Cuthbert William, *The Life of Sir Edward Coke.* 2 vols. 2nd ed. London, 1845. There is much need of a more scholarly biography of Sir Edward Coke.

Kennedy, William, *English Taxation 1640-1799. An essay on Policy and Opinion* (London School of Economics and Political Science Series, No. XXXII). London, 1913. Brief but useful.

Lapsley, Thomas Gaillard, *County Palatine of Durham: a Study in Constitutional History* (Harvard Historical Studies, VIII). New York, 1900.

Morris, W. A., *The Early English County Court* (University of California Publications in History, XIV, No. 2). Berkeley, 1926. A very considerable addition to previous knowledge of the subject derived from Stubbs and Maitland.

——— *The Mediaeval English Sheriff to 1300.* Manchester University Press, 1927.

Pollock, Sir Frederick, and Maitland, Frederic William, *The History of English Law Before the Time of Edward I.* 2 vols. 2nd ed. Cambridge, 1898.

Sweet and Maxwell, *Bibliography of English Law to 1650.* London, 1925.

Webb, Sidney, and Beatrice, *English Local Government from the Revolution to the Municipal Corporations Act: the Parish and the County.* New York, 1906. Contains helpful notes on local institutions of the earlier period as well.

Winfield, Percy H., *The Chief Sources of English Legal History.* Based on a course of lectures delivered in the Law School of Harvard University, February-June, 1923. Harvard University Press, 1925.

B. CONTEMPORANEOUS SOURCES

1. Unpublished Material

Assizes, Order Books. Assizes 24/20, Order Book, 1629-41; 24/21, 1641-52; 24/22, 1652-76; 35/82, 1640. Public Record Office.

Chetham Manuscripts and Memoirs. Chetham Library, Manchester.

Durham Judgment Rolls, 13/36, *rot.* 19-20; 13/15, *rot.* 2-2d; 13/26, *rot.* 18-18d. Public Record Office.

Exchequer—King's Remembrancer: List of Sheriffs' Accounts. Bundles 14/33 and 60/15. Public Record Office.

Harleian Manuscripts, CLX and CLXV. British Museum.

Kenyon Manuscripts. Gredington Hall, Flintshire. Uncalendared. Scattered information of value on the sheriff's duties and on manorial courts not calendared by the visiting Records Commission. *See* Historical Manuscripts Commission.

Lancashire Indictments, Quarter-Sessions, 1657. Sessions House, Preston, Lancashire.

Lancaster Sessions Rolls. Sessions House, Preston, Lancashire. Contain a wealth of information on the proceedings in quarter-sessions.

Partington Manuscripts, Military Annals of Lancaster. Chetham Library, Manchester.

Raines Manuscripts, XXIII. Chetham Library, Manchester.

Sheriff's Lists of Grand Juries, 1627-28. Sessions House, Preston, Lancashire.

Star Chamber Proceedings, James I. Bundles 209/21, 217/16, 304/32, 118/9, 54/15, 15/26. Public Record Office.

2. PUBLISHED MATERIAL

a. Publications Issued by the Government

Acts and Ordinances of the Interregnum, 1642-1660. Collected and edited by C. H. Firth and R. S. Rait. 3 vols. London, 1911.

Acts of the Privy Council. Vols. 1601-04, 1613-14.

Calendar of State Papers, Domestic. Volumes for the period 1603 to 1689.

Deputy Keeper of the Rolls, Public Records, *Reports; Lists and Indexes,* No. IX.

Historical Manuscripts Commission, *Reports.* Principally the Kenyon Manuscripts.

Journals of the House of Commons.

Journals of the House of Lords.

Kenyon Manuscripts. Historical Manuscripts Commission.

Lists and Indexes, No. IX. *See* Deputy Keeper of the Rolls.

Rutland Manuscripts. Historical Manuscripts Commission.

Second and Final Report of the Commissioners Appointed to Inquire into the Course of Proceedings in Suits, &c. in the Courts of the County Palatine of Lancaster, 1836.
Statutes of the Realm.

b. Published Court Records

Coke's Reports. (K. B., C. P., Exch., etc., 1572-1616).

Cox, Rev. J. Charles, *Three Centuries of Derbyshire Annals. As Illustrated by the records of the quarter-sessions of the County of Derby from Queen Elizabeth to Queen Victoria.* 2 vols. London, 1890.

Hamilton, A. H. A., *Quarter-Sessions from Queen Elizabeth to Queen Anne. Illustrations of local government and history drawn from original sources, chiefly of Devon.* London, 1878.

Lancashire Quarter-Sessions Records, 1590-1606. Edited by J. Tait (Chetham Society Publications, New Series, LXXVII). Manchester, 1917.

Manchester Sessions. Edited by Ernest Axon (Lancashire and Cheshire Record Society Publications, XLII). London, 1901.

Middlesex County Records. Edited by J. C. Jeaffreson (Middlesex County Record Society Publications, I-IV). London, 1886-92.

North Riding of the County of York Quarter-Sessions Records. Edited by the Rev. J. C. Atkinson (North Riding Record Society Publications, I-VII). London, 1884-89.

Quarter-Sessions Records of the County of Northampton A. D. 1630, 1657, 1657-8. Edited by Joan Wake. (Northamptonshire Record Society Publications, Vol. I). Hereford, 1924.

Quarter-Sessions Records for the County of Somerset. Edited by the Rev. E. H. B. Harbin; the last volume by M. C. B. Dawes (Somerset Record Society Publications, XXIII, XXIV, XXVIII, XXXIV). London, 1907-19.

West Riding Sessions Records. Edited by John Lister (Yorkshire Archaeological Society Publications, III and LIV). London, 1888, 1915.

Worcestershire County Records, Calendar of the Quarter-Sessions Papers, I, 1591-1643. Compiled for the Records and Charities Committee by J. W. Willis Bund. Worcester, 1900. The introduction contains a valuable description of the organization, procedure, and business of quarter-sessions.

c. *Biographies, Diaries, Journals, Letters and Miscellaneous Collections of Sources*

Autobiography of Sir John Bramston. Edited by R. G. Neville (Camden Society Publications, First Series, XXXII). London, 1845.

Autobiography and Correspondence of Sir Simonds D'Ewes. Edited by J. O. Halliwell. 2 vols. London, 1845.

Cheshire Notes and Queries, New Series, vol. of 1888. Stockport, England.

The Cheshire Sheaf, Chester, 1883-86.

Christie, W. D., *A Life of Anthony Ashley Cooper, First Earl of Shaftesbury.* 2 vols. London, 1871.

The Constitutional Documents of The Puritan Revolution, 1625-1660. Edited by S. R. Gardiner. 3rd ed., revised. London, 1906.

Devon and Cornwall Notes and Gleanings. Vol. II. Exeter, 1889.

Diary of Henry Townshend of Elmley Lovett, 1640-1663. Edited by J. W. Willis Bund for the Worcestershire Historical Society. 4 vols., 1915-20. Valuable information on the military and financial arrangements of the civil war period.

Diary of John Evelyn. Edited by H. B. Wheatley. 4 vols. London, 1906.

Diary of the Rev. Ralph Josselin, 1616-1683. Edited for the Royal Historical Society by E. Hockliffe (Camden Society Publications, Third Series, XV). London, 1908.

The Earl of Strafforde's Letters and Dispatches. Edited by William Knowler. With an essay toward his life by Sir George Radcliffe. 2 vols. London, 1739.

The Egerton Papers. A Collection of Public and Private Documents Chiefly Illustrative of the Times of Elizabeth and James I. Edited by J. Payne Collier (Camden Society Publications, First Series, XII). London, 1840.
Evelyn, John. *See* Diary of.
Gloucestershire Notes and Queries. Vol. V. London, 1894.
Hutchinson, William, *The History and Antiquities of the County Palatine of Durham.* 2 vols. Newcastle, 1785-87.
Josselin, Rev. Ralph. *See* Diary of.
The Journal of Sir Simonds D'Ewes from the Beginning of the Long Parliament to the Opening of the Trial of the Earl of Strafford. Edited by Wallace Notestein. New Haven, Yale University Press, 1923.
Lancashire and Cheshire Record Society Publications. Vol. XII. 1885.
Life of Humphrey Chetham. Edited by Francis Robert Raines and Charles W. Sutton, with genealogy of Chetham family by Ernest Axon (Chetham Society Publications, New Series, XLIX and L). Manchester, 1903.
Memoirs and Travels of Sir John Reresby, Bart. Edited by A. Ivatt. London, 1904.
Northamptonshire Notes and Queries. Vol. I. Northampton, 1886-87.
Prothero, G. W., *Select Statutes and other Constitutional Documents of the Reigns of Elizabeth and James I., 1559-1625.* 2nd ed. London, The Clarendon Press, 1898.
The Shrievalty of William Ffarington, Esq., 1636. Edited by Susan Maria Ffarington (Chetham Society Publications, Old Series, XXXIX). Manchester, 1856.
Somerset and Dorset Notes and Queries. Vol. VII. Sherborne, 1901.
Tanner, J. R., *Tudor Constitutional Documents A. D. 1485-1603, with an Historical Commentary.* Cambridge, 1922. Useful source materials for local government, in particular for the Tudor justice of the peace.
Townshend, Henry. *See* Diary of.
Tracts Relating to Military Proceedings in Lancashire During the Great Civil War. Edited and illustrated from contemporary documents by George Ormerod (Chetham Society Publications, Old Series, II). Manchester, 1844.

d. Legal Treatises

Coke, Sir Edward, *Institutes of the Laws of England.* First part of Commentary upon Littleton, fol. 1628. Second, third, and fourth parts published after the author's death, 1642-44. The fourth part takes up the jurisdiction of the courts.

Dalton, Michael, *The Countrey Justice: containing the Practice of the Justice of the Peace Out of their Sessions, to which is now added the Duty and Power of Justices of the Peace in their sessions.* 1677. First edition, 1618.

Dalton, Michael, *Officium Vicecomitum or the Office and Authorities of Sheriffs.* 1623.

Fitzherbert, Sir Anthonie, *Loffice et aucthoritie de Justices de peace A que est annex Loffice de Vicecomites, Baylifes, Escheators, Constables, Coroners, etc.* Enlarged by, and known as, "Crompton." 1583.

Fortescue, Sir John, *De Laudibus Legum Angliae.* Written about 1468. A very early, if not first, edition printed in 1616.

Greenwood, William, *Curia Comitatus Rediviva, or the Pratique Part of the County-Court revived.* 1657.

———— *A Practical Demonstration of County-judicatures wherein is explained the judicial and ministerial authority of Sheriffs and Coroners.* 1659.

Hale, Sir Matthew, *A Short Treatise Touching Sheriff's Accompts* (1683). Bound in Hale's *Pleas of the Crown.* 1716.

Smith, Sir Thomas, *De Republica Anglorum. The Maner of Government, or Policie of the Realme of England.* 1583. Exposition of the political and legal constitution of England in the reign of Elizabeth.

Wilkinson, J., *Treatise collected out of the statutes of the Kingdom and according to common experience of the Lawes concerning the Office and Authoritie of Coroners and Sherifes, with an easie method for the keeping of a Court Leet, Court Baron, and Hundred Court, etc.* 1618.

Note: The above dates are those of the first editions. The legal textbooks cited describe the county officials and the county courts according to the law and are not in all particulars safe as regards the practice.

II. VIRGINIA

A. NON-CONTEMPORANEOUS ACCOUNTS, BIBLIOGRAPHIES, AND GUIDES

Beverley, Robert, *History and Present State of Virginia.* First edition, 1705.

Bond, Beverley W., *The Quit-Rent System in the American Colonies.* Introduction by Charles M. Andrews. New Haven, Yale University Press, 1919.

Bruce, Philip Alexander, *Economic History of Virginia in the Seventeenth Century.* 2 vols. New York, 1895. Reprint, 1907. An exhaustive study of much value.

——— *Institutional History of Virginia in the Seventeenth Century. An Inquiry into the Religious, Moral, Educational, Legal, Military, and Political Condition of the People Based on Original and Contemporaneous Sources.* 2 vols. New York, 1910. The only thorough study of the local institutions of Virginia in this period that has been made. Written in a very interesting manner. The bibliography is uncritical; the titles too brief.

——— *Social Life of Virginia in the Seventeenth Century.* Richmond, 1907. Does not measure up to his other works on this period.

——— *History of Virginia: Colonial Period 1607-1763.* The first volume of a six-volume work on the *History of Virginia* by P. A. Bruce, L. G. Tyler, Richard L. Morton, and others. P. A. Bruce, editor-in-chief. American Historical Society, New York, 1924. Supersedes the general works by Campbell (1860), Cooke (1883), and other writers on the colonial period. Bibliography is uncritical; titles of work consulted are incomplete.

Chandler, J. A. C., *The History of Suffrage in Virginia* (Johns Hopkins University Studies, Series XIX, Nos. 6-7). 1901.

——— *Representation in Virginia* (Johns Hopkins University Studies, Series XIV, Nos. 6-7). 1896. Useful, though not final.

Chitwood, O. P., *Justice in Colonial Virginia* (Johns Hopkins University Studies, Series XXIII, Nos. 7-8). 1905. Helpful, though many of the county court orders of the 17th century were not examined.

Colonial Virginia Register. A List of Governors, Councillors and other Higher Officials, and also of Members of the House of Burgesses, and the Revolutionary Conventions of the Colony of Virginia. Compiled by W. G. and M. N. Stanard. Albany, 1902.

Flippin, Percy Scott, *The Financial Administration of the Colony of Virginia* (Johns Hopkins University Studies, Series XXXIII, No. 2). 1915. Scholarly.

────── *The Royal Government in Virginia, 1624-1775* (Columbia University Studies in History, Economics, and Public Law, LXXXIV, No. 1). 1918. Extensive bibliography.

Handbook of Manuscripts in the Library of Congress. Washington, 1918.

Howard, G. E., *An Introduction to the Local Constitutional History of the United States* (Johns Hopkins University Studies, extra Vol. IV). 1889.

Ingle, Edward, *Local Institutions of Virginia* (Johns Hopkins University Studies, Series III, Nos. 2-3). 1885. Out of date.

Justices of the Peace of Colonial Virginia 1757-1775. Edited by H. R. McIlwaine, Virginia State Librarian (Bulletin of the Virginia State Library, Vol. XIV, Nos. 2 and 3). Richmond, 1921.

Kennedy, John P., *Virginia State Library Calendar of Transcripts, 1573-1772.* Annual report of the Department of Archives and History. Richmond, 1905. Decidedly inaccurate and not up to date.

Osgood, H. L., *The American Colonies in the Seventeenth Century.* 3 vols. New York, 1904-7.

Robinson, Morgan P., *Virginia Counties: Those Resulting from Virginia Legislation.* (Bulletin of the Virginia State Library, Vol. IX, Nos. 1-3.) Richmond, 1916. Much useful information on the formation of counties in Virginia. Well illustrated with maps.

Stith, William, *The History of the First Discovery and Settlement of Virginia.* Sabin reprint, New York, 1865. Index to various editions of Stith prepared by Morgan P. Robinson, Virginia State Archivist (Bulletin of the Virginia State Library, Vol. V). Richmond, 1912.

Swem, E. G., *A Bibliography of Virginia.* 3 parts. Richmond, 1916-19.

Tyler, Lyon Gardiner, *The Cradle of the Republic, Jamestown and James River.* 2nd ed. Richmond, 1906.

Wertenbaker, T. J., *The Planters of Colonial Virginia.* Princeton University Press, 1922. On the basis of the rent roll of 1704 contests Bruce's thesis that the planters and not the yeomen were the most important social, political, and economic factors in seventeenth-century Virginia.

B. CONTEMPORANEOUS SOURCES

1. UNPUBLISHED MATERIAL

Colonial Office, Class 5, Vols. 1376 and 1405. Transcripts of documents in the Public Record Office. Now printed in the *Executive Journals of the Council of Colonial Virginia.* Vol. I, June 11, 1680-June 22, 1699, and Vol. II, August 3, 1699-April 27, 1705. Edited by H. R. McIlwaine, Virginia State Librarian. Richmond, 1925, 1927.

County Court Records:

Accomac County Records. Vols. 1632-40, 1640-45, certified copies, Virginia State Library; Vols. 1663-66, 1666-70, 1671-73, 1676-78, 1678-82, 1682-97, originals, clerk's office, Accomac, Va.

Charles City County Records. Vol. 1655-65, original, Virginia State Library.

Henrico County Records. Vol. 1677-92, original; Vol. 1682-1701, certified copy. Original and certified copy, Virginia State Library.

Lancaster County Records. Vols. 1652-57, 1655-66, 1666-80, 1680-86, 1686-96. Clerk's office, Lancaster, Va.

Lower Norfolk County Records. Vols. 1637-46, 1646-51, 1651-56, 1656-66, 1666-75, 1675-86, 1686-95. Clerk's office, Portsmouth, Va.

Middlesex County Records. Vols. 1673-80, 1680-94. Clerk's office, Saluda, Va.

Northampton County Records. Vols. 1645-51, 1651-54, 1654-55, 1655-56, 1657-64, 1664-74, 1674-79, 1679-83, 1683-89. Clerk's office, Eastville, Va.

Northumberland County Records, Order Books. Vols. 1652-65, 1666-78, 1678-98, originals, Virginia State Library.

Rappahannock County Records. Vols. 1683-86, 1686-92, certified copies, Virginia State Library.

Stafford County Records. Vol. 1664-68. Stafford, Va.

Surry County Records. Vol. 1645-72, certified copy, Virginia State Library; Vol. 1671-90, Surry, Va.

Westmoreland County Records. Vols. 1662-64, 1675/6-1688/9. Clerk's office, Montross, Va.

York County Records. Vols. 1638-48, 1657-62, 1664-72, 1671-94, 1675-84, 1684-87, 1687-91, certified copies, Virginia State Library.

Note: Only the court orders of the county court records listed above were consulted. A number of the volumes marked "deeds" contained court orders either scattered among the deeds or reserved to themselves in the front or back of the volume.

Edmund Randolph Manuscript. Journal of the Council and Assembly, 1626-1634. Division of Manuscripts, Library of Congress.

Randolph Manuscripts. 3 vols. Virginia Historical Society, Richmond. A copy of the Bland Manuscript in the Division of Manuscripts, Library of Congress.

Sainsbury Papers, 1606-1740. 20 vols. Virginia State Library. Transcripts and abstracts of documents in the Public Record Office relating to Virginia. Abstracts are too brief to be of much value.

Virginia Company Records. Vol. II (1621-26). Division of Manuscripts, Library of Congress.

BIBLIOGRAPHY

Virginia Miscellaneous Papers, 1606-80. Division of Manuscripts, Library of Congress.

Winder Papers. Transcripts of documents in the British Archives. Vol. I, 1607-76; Vol. II, Bacon's Rebellion. Virginia State Library.

Note: Numerous extracts from the county records, from the Sainsbury Abstracts, and the Winder Papers have been printed in the *Virginia Magazine of History and Biography* and in other historical and genealogical periodicals of Virginia.

2. PUBLISHED RECORDS OF THE COLONIAL GOVERNMENT

Executive Journals of the Council of Colonial Virginia. Vols. I-III, 1680-1721. Edited by H. R. McIlwaine, Virginia State Librarian. Richmond, 1925, 1927, 1928.

Hening, W. W., *The Statutes-at-Large, being a collection of all the Laws of Virginia* (1619-1792). 13 vols. Philadelphia and New York, 1823.

Journals of the House of Burgesses of Virginia. Vols. 1619-1658/9, 1659/60-1693. Edited by H. R. McIlwaine. Virginia State Library, Richmond, 1914, 1915.

Minutes of the Council and General Court of Colonial Virginia, 1622-1632, 1670-1676. With Notes and Excerpts from Original Council and General Court Records, into 1683, now lost. Edited by H. R. McIlwaine. Virginia State Library, Richmond, 1924.

3. PERIODICALS AND MISCELLANEOUS COLLECTIONS OF SOURCES

Brown, Alexander, *The First Republic in America.* Boston, 1898.

—— *The Genesis of the United States.* Boston, 1890.

Calendar of Virginia State Papers (1652-1793). 6 vols. Edited by W. P. Palmer. Virginia State Library, Richmond, 1875-76.

Collections of the Virginia Historical Society. New Series, Vols. 1-11. Richmond, 1833-1892. Place taken by the *Virginia Magazine of History and Biography.*

Force, Peter, *Tracts and other Papers relating principally to the Origin, Settlement, and Progress of the Colonies in North America from the discovery of the Country to the year 1776.* Collected by Peter Force. 4 vols. Washington, 1836-46.

Hartwell, Chilton, and Blair, *An Account of the Present State and Government of Virginia.* Probably written in England about 1698. Reprinted in the *Massachusetts Historical Society Collections,* Series I, Vol. V.

Lower Norfolk County Virginia Antiquary. Edited by E. W. James. 5 vols. Richmond and Baltimore, 1895-1906.

Virginia Magazine of History and Biography. Published by the Virginia Historical Society. Editor, W. G. Stanard. 1892 to date. Contains extracts from the records of the central and local governments that are helpful to the student of the political institutions of colonial Virginia.

William and Mary College Quarterly Historical and Genealogical Magazine. 27 vols. Williamsburg and Richmond, 1892-1919. Discontinued with the April number of 1919 and now known as the *William and Mary College Quarterly Historical Magazine.* Edited by J. A. C. Chandler and E. G. Swem of William and Mary College.

III. MARYLAND

A. NON-CONTEMPORANEOUS ACCOUNTS

Bozman, John Leeds, *The History of Maryland from its first settlement in 1633, to the Restoration in 1660, etc.* 2 vols. Baltimore, 1837.

Browne, W. H., *Maryland, the History of a Palatinate.* Revised and enlarged edition, Boston, 1904. A general political and social history.

Hanson, G. A., *Old Kent: The Eastern Shore of Maryland.* Baltimore, 1876. Largely genealogical, but contains a number of interesting extracts from county and parish records.

Kilty, J., *The Land-Holder's Assistant and Land Office Guide.* Baltimore, 1808.

INDEX

Accomac County, 67, 68, 69, 70, 73, 81n, 100.
Allerton, Colonel Isaac, offices held by, 69-70.
Ann Arundel County, 84, 85, 91.
Arlington, 10, 112.
Assembly, combining of offices prohibited by, 80; composition of in early Maryland, 123-24; control of over poll taxes, 130-33; dismemberment of prevented by, 72; number of burgesses elected to, 120-21; public levy apportioned by, 132; service of warrants at musters and county courts prohibited by, 102; sheriff denied membership in, 88; term in office conditioned by, 88; suffrage restricted by, 120.
Assizes, administrative work at, 20-21, 26-27; description of procession to, 186-87; entertainment by sheriff at, 25-26; limitation of cost of, 26; organization of by sheriff, 17; selection of chaplain for, 27-28; Sheriff's Table at, 27, 36; social preëminence of sheriff at, 23-25.
Auditor, 137.
Auditor-general, 144.

Bacon's Laws, 80.
Bailiffs, appointment of by sheriff, 11, 47; dishonesty of, 18-19, 51-52; duties of in county court, 48-49.
Baltemore County, 85, 102, 105.
Basse, Nathaniel, 66, 194-96.
Benevolences, 54-55.
Berkeley, Governor, appointment of sheriff certified by, 78; arbitrary appointments of, 76, 79, 146; harsh treatment of Quakers by, 149-50.
Book of Orders, 35.

Calvert, Cecilius, 82; Charles, 122; Leonard, 82.
Calvert County, 85, 102.
Casual revenues of the crown, 53, 138, 192-93.
Cecil County, formation of, 85; sheriff of impeached, 89; sheriff summoned by coroner of, 189-90.

Chancery, return of writ of election to, 31; *dedimus* to justices of the peace, 10; of Durham, 45.
Charles City County, 69, 75n, 79, 105, 138.
Charles County, 84, 85, 91, 102, 103.
Chetham, Humphrey, collector of ship-money, 56-58, 58n; efforts of to escape shrievalty, 8-9; in procession to assizes, 24; loyalty of to Parliament, 6; recommendation of subordinates to, 11-12.
Churchwardens, as collectors of parish levies, 134.
Coke, Sir Edward, objection of to oath of office, 14-15; removal of from Parliament, 5.
Colonial divergencies from England, general, 152-59; in colonial courts, 106-13.
Commander, as president of county court, 65; as election official in Virginia, 118, 128; in Maryland, 125, 128-29; commission of, 194-96; decline of, 84; provost-marshal appointed by, 66; sheriff in Maryland appointed by, 91.
Commissioners of the county court. *See* justices of the peace (colonial).
Communication, governmental, between central and local gov't., in England, 30, in Maryland, 121-22, in Virginia, 114-15; within the county, in England, 29-30, in Maryland, 121-22, in Virginia, 114.
Compositions for knighthood, 56.
Composition money, 142.
Compurgation, 46-47.
Conquest, Richard, as executive officer of vestry, 114n; dealings of with non-conformists, 148-49; declaration of deodand before, 138-39.
Constables, as assessors and collectors in England, 57; as election officials in Maryland, 124, 125, 127, 129; oath of office of, 197; tithables listed by, 131n, 140.
Cooper, Anthony Ashley, justice of the peace and sheriff, 4; retinue at assizes, 24.

INDEX

Coroners, command of over sheriff, 189-90; duties of in Maryland, 86-87; early performed by sheriff in colonies, 79-80, 86; elected in county court in England, 48; outlawry declared by, 48n; to recover casual revenues, 138, 192-93.

Council, colonial gentry appointed to, 68-70, 87; dispute over appointment in, 89-90; functions of in Maryland, 83; nominations of, 90; sheriff appointed by governor and council, 72-73.

Country gentry, monopoly of over county offices, in England 3-4, in Maryland 87-88, in Virginia 68-71; rotation of office among, 70, 92, 188.

County clerk, appointed in England by sheriff, 11; candidacy for office of, 12; colonial office of combined with shrievalty, 74-75, 78, 79; copies of statutes secured by, 115n; duties of in Maryland, 87; in sheriff's county court, 48n, 51; fees of collected by sheriff, 136; meagreness of records of, 106; oath of, 196; rent rolls revised by, 142; tithables recorded by, 130, 131.

County court in England, 37-52; defects of, 50-52; election in, 31-32; jurisdiction of, 49-50; out of place in colonies, 113; sheriff as chairman and executive of, 46-49; small profits of, 53n; statutes published in, 30; suitors as judges in, 40-43, 45, 46, 47; writs of election published in, 115.

County court in the colonies, as Orphans' Court, 96-97; comparison of with English county court, 107; with quarter sessions, 107-8; early called "monthly courts" in Virginia, 64-65; early commissioners of, 66; elections held in, 127; justice speedier and cheaper in, 112-13; organization of by sheriff, 94-98; pleadings in simplified, 112; procedure modeled after England, 110-12, proclamations in, 116-17, 122, 126; respect for magistrates of enforced by, 104-6; sessions of in Virginia, 95-96; sheriff as administrative official of, 99-101; as chief executive official of, 98-99, 102-4, writs of election cried in, 126.

County leadership of sheriff, 23, 92, 158.

Court crier, 81, 141.

Custis, John, 69, 99n.

Dale, Major Edward, 79, 106.

Dale's Laws, 63, 64.

Dalton's *Office of Sheriff*, 3, 111.

D'Ewes, Sir Simonds, election worries of, 33-34; judges of assizes met by, 23.

Deodands, one of casual revenues, 53; nature of in the colonies, 138-39, 143, 193-94.

Dorchester County, 85, 92, 105.

Durham, Bishop of, 6-7, 82.

Durham, county court of, 38, 43, 44.

Elizabeth City County, 133.

Ellesmere, Lord, 5, 12.

Escheator, sheriff in capacity of, 142-43.

Evelyn, John, 4, 24-25.

Exchequer, casual revenues accounted at, 53; discharge out of, 144; expense of accounting at, 3, 151; loans paid into, 55; nominations for sheriff in, 7.

Exchequer, Chester court of, 50.

Exigentur, duties of, 12n.

Ffarington, William, fined by judges, 23-24; household help of at assizes, 25-26; oath of office of, 165-67.

Fitzhugh, William, 108-9.

Forced Loans, 55-56.

Forfeitures, 137. *See also* Casual revenues of the crown.

Fort duty, 136.

General Court, criminals tried by, 109-10; description of sheriff's office by, 93; early jurisdiction and functions of, 64; simplified procedure in, 112, 113.

Gloucester, statute of, 37.

Governor, appointment of sheriff by, 73, 78, 91; election duties of, 118, 123, 125, 127.

Grievances against the sheriff, 32, 76-77, 79-80, 88-89, 129, 131.

INDEX 217

Harvey, Governor, 68, 100.
Hill, Colonel Edward, offices held by, 69, 75n.
Horsey, Stephen, offices held by, 88n.
Hue and cry, 147-48, 197.
Hundreds, as units of assessment and collection in England, 57; of representation in early Virginia, 117; importance of in local government of England, 59, of Maryland 85-86; tithables listed and assessments in Maryland made by, 140, 141; significance of in election system of Maryland, 122-28.

Jailer, bond of to sheriff, 13, 169; duties and fees of in Virginia, 81.
James, Charles, impeachment of, 89.
James City County, 95n.
Jamestown, 66, 70n, 80, 93, 110, 114, 115, 117, 118, 120, 121, 122, 144, 157, 158, 196.
Juries, different organization of in Virginia, 110; freehold books for, 17-18; impanelling of by sheriff, 17-18, 97-98; in sheriff's county court, 40, 44, 46-47; of appraisal, 100-1; jury trial in the colonies, 109-10; wages fixed by, 29.
Justices of the peace (England), administrative duties of at assizes, 21, at quarter-sessions, 20-21, at Sheriff's Table, 27, 36; appointment of country gentry to, 3-4; as suitors in the county court, 39, 42; associations of with sheriff, 21-22, 158; bond and sheriff's oaths taken by, 10; commission of, 179-83; contributions to royal revenues from, 54; freehold books drawn up by, 17-18; reports on local conditions by, 34-35; social inferiority of to sheriff, 23.
Justices of the peace (colonial), administrative duties of, 100, 101; alternation of planters between justices and sheriff, 68-71, 88; as commissioners over monthly courts, 64-65; association of with commander, 83-84; commission of (Maryland), 183-86; control over appointment of sheriff, 76, 77-79; county levy pro-rated by, 132, 141; election of sheriff ordered by, 74; extent of judicial authority of, 107; importance of in county government, 108; induction of sheriff by, 75, 91; legal responsibility of for taxes, 134, 157; lists of tithables examined by, 130, 131, 140; offices of in colonies similar, 86; recommendation of sheriff by, 88, 89; respect for magistrates enforced by, 104-6; sessions of county court held by, 95-96; warrant of to summon sessions, 177-79.
Justicies, writ of, 37, 45, 47, 49, 50.

Kent, Isle and County of, commander of, 83-84, 125; dispute over sheriff of, 89; election official of, 125, 128-29, 156; military command to sheriff of, 188-89; respect for magistrates enforced in, 104; sheriff of fined, 102; writ of election to, 124n.

Lancashire, sheriffs of, 6, 8, 14, 35, 56; justices of, 36; county court in, 41.
Lancaster County, 74, 79, 106, 133, 147.
Langley, Captain Ralph, 77-78.
Laws of Virginia, divergencies of from English laws, 108-9.
Lawson, Colonel Anthony, offices held by, 70-71.
Lear, Lieut. Colonel, monopoly of offices of, 77n.
Lord-lieutenant, 3, 22.
Lower Norfolk County, 68, 71, 95, 96, 105, 114n, 138, 148, 149.
Ludwell, Thomas, 112, 144.

Manorial courts, temporary, 113.
Mattapanient hundred, 83, 115.
Mellinge, William, 77, 78, 79.
Middlesex County, 70, 81, 133, 135.
Middleton Case, 38-42.
Military command to sheriff, in England, 22-23; in Maryland, 188-89.

Monthly courts. *See* County court (colonial).
Morgan, John, offices held by, 88n.

Nansemond County, 77n.
Northampton County, 69, 74, 77, 78, 79, 81, 95, 99n, 101, 133, 137, 148, 193-94.
Northumberland County, 69.

Oaths, of colonial sheriff, 75, 93, 167-68, 168-69; of constable, 197; of county clerk, 196; of English sheriff, 14-15, 165-67; of sheriff taken before justices, 10, 75, 91.
Orphans' Court, 96-97.

Parish, election of vestry supervised by sheriff, 175-76; levies of, 134; representation of, 117, 120; salary of delegate of collected by sheriff, 174-75.
Parke, Captain Daniel, offices held by, 69.
Parliament, appointment of sheriff by, 7; as temporary treasurer for, 36; collection of grants of, 58-59; elections of 1640, 33-34; financial struggle with King, 54; military command to sheriff by order of, 22-23; relief from shrievalty sought of, 4, 8-9; sheriff craves pardon of, 32.
Patent of sheriff's office, in England, 7, 10, 163; in Maryland, 91; in Virginia, 75, 163-64.
Philips, John, sheriff and clerk, 74-75.
Police powers of sheriff, 21-22, 147-150, 176-77.
Poll taxes, assessment of, 140; collection of, 132-34, 141, 145; fees of collectors of, 135-36, 141; items of county levy of, 141; justices pro-rate, 132; listing of tithables in Virginia, 130-31; by sheriff and constables in Maryland, 139-40; warrant to take lists for, 190.
Posse comitatus, use of in emergency, 22, 147; warrant for summoning of, 176-77.
Prisons, description of in Virginia, 150-51; in sheriff's charge, 13.
Privy Council, collection of royal revenues under supervision of, 54-57; local administration supervised by, 34-35; nominees of for sheriff, 7, 7n; order of concerning chaplain of assizes, 27-28.
Proclamations, by sheriff throughout county, 29-31; in county court, 31, 115, 116, 126, 172-73; of new proprietor, 122; of new ruler, 116-17, 122; publishing of governor's proclamations, 115.
Proprietor, powers of, 82; revenues of, 141-43.
Provincial Court, constitution of, 83; county court united with, 84-85; sheriffs fined by, 102.
Provost-marshal, appointment of by commander, 66; as military official, 64; as appraiser, 100; duties and fees of, 65-67; forerunner of sheriff, 64-65, 87.
Punishments, colonial methods of, 103-5; greater leniency of in colonies, 109n.
Purchase money, 142.

Quakers, county magistrates to disperse, 21-22; ill-treatment of by Berkeley, 149-50.
Qualifications and appointment of sheriff, in England, 3-13; in Maryland, 81-92; in Virginia, 63-81.
Quarter-sessions, administrative duties of sheriff at, 20-21; comparison of with colonial county court, 107-8; executive duties of sheriff at, 18-20, infrequent attendance of sheriff at, 16-17; orders of proclaimed by sheriff, 29-30; organization by sheriff, 16; warrant to sheriff to summon, 177-79.
Quit-rents, in Maryland, 142; in Virginia, 136-37.

Receiver-general, 142, 143.
Representation, early Maryland assemblies, how constituted, 124; elections to Parliament, 30-31; elections manipulated by sheriff, 32; election officials in Maryland, 123-27; election responsibilities of sheriff in colonies, 117-21, 128; election worries in

INDEX 219

England, 33-34; franchise in Virginia, 119-20; number of burgesses, 120-21; proclamations of election, 126-27; system of compared with English, 128-29; units of in Maryland, 122-26; in Virginia, 117, 120, 128. *See also* Assembly and Writs of election.
Reresby, Sir John, entertainment by at assizes, 25; shrievalty sought by, 9-10.
Robins, Captain John, loyalty to Berkeley rewarded, 79.
Rotation of office, 188. *See also* Country gentry.

St. Clement's hundred, 125.
St. George's hundred, 83, 125, 127.
St. Mary's, 82, 83, 84, 85, 91-92, 102n, 103, 110, 121, 122, 123, 124n, 125, 126, 127, 128, 129, 140, 141, 144, 155, 157, 186, 189.
St. Mary's hundred, 83, 125, 127.
St. Michael's hundred, 125, 127.
Scarborough, Colonel Edmund, offices held by, 70.
Secretary, 91, 117, 118, 126, 128, 136, 141.
Sheriff's Table, administrative work at, 27, 36.
Ship-money, collection of, 56-58.
Sibsey, Captain John, offices held by, 68-69.
Somerset County in England, 3-4, 18, 20-21, 29; in Maryland, 85, 190.
Stafford County, 147, 151.
Star Chamber, Court of, 43, 51.
Stone, Captain William, offices held by, 67, 69; contract of with under-sheriff, 80-81; nomination of for sheriff, 73.
Suitors of the county court. *See* County court (England).
Surry County, 69.

Surveyor, 68, 70, 77n, 80n, 88n, 122.
Swann, Colonel Thomas, offices held by, 69.
Sweatnam, Edward, case of, 89-90; justices notice disrespect to, 105.

Talbot County, 85, 126, 143, 191.
Taylor, Major, 92.
Treasure trove. *See* Casual revenues of the crown.
Treasurer, 58, 89, 136.

Under-sheriff, appointment, duties, and fees of in England, 12-13; in Maryland, 91-92; in Virginia, 80-81; dishonesty of, 18-19, 51; duties of sheriff executed by, 5, 17; early called "bailiff" in St. Mary's, 91-92; legal requirements of in England, 12; of lower social class, 13; period of in office limited, 6, 13, 76, 88.

Vaughan, Robert, high constable, 87n.

Waters, William, elected sheriff, 74.
Wentworth, Sir Thomas, excluded from Parliament, 5; servant of for under-sheriff, 12.
Westmoreland County, 70, 95.
Wormeley, Colonel Christopher, offices held by, 70.
Writs, of assistance, 11, 22, 91, 164; of discharge, 11, 187-88; of election, 30-31, 117, 118, 119, 124n, 125-26, 128, 170-72, 172-74; judicial, 18, 99, 102-103, 191-92.

Yeardley, Governor, 65, 194.
York County, 68, 69, 77, 78, 116-17, 137, 149, 188.